# foundations

## SMALL GROUP STUDY

taught by tom holladay and kay warren

# HOLY SPIRIT

ZONDERVAN®

SADDLEBACK CHURCH

ZONDERVAN.com/
AUTHORTRACKER
*follow your favorite authors*

Foundations: *Holy Spirit Study Guide*
Copyright © 2004, 2008 by Tom Holladay and Kay Warren

Requests for information should be addressed to:
Zondervan, *Grand Rapids, Michigan 49530*

ISBN 978-0-310-27676-0

08 09 10 11 12 13 14 15 16 17 18 • 23 22 21 20 19 18 17 16 15 14 13 12 11 10 9 8 7 6 5 4 3 2 1

## FOREWORD

### What *Foundations* Will Do for You

I once built a log cabin in the Sierra Mountains of northern California. After ten backbreaking weeks of clearing forest land, all I had to show for my effort was a leveled and squared concrete foundation. I was discouraged, but my father, who built over a hundred church buildings in his lifetime, said, "Cheer up, son! Once you've laid the foundation, the most important work is behind you." I've since learned that this is a principle for all of life: you can never build *anything* larger than the foundation can handle.

The foundation of any building determines both its size and strength, and the same is true of our lives. A life built on a false or faulty foundation will never reach the height that God intends for it to reach. If you skimp on your foundation, you limit your life.

That's why this material is so vitally important. *Foundations* is the biblical basis of a purpose-driven life. You must understand these life-changing truths to enjoy God's purposes for you. This curriculum has been taught, tested, and refined over ten years with thousands of people at Saddleback Church. I've often said that *Foundations* is the most important class in our church.

### Why You Need a Biblical Foundation for Life

- *It's the source of personal growth and stability.* So many of the problems in our lives are caused by faulty thinking. That's why Jesus said the truth will set us free and why Colossians 2:7a (CEV) says, *"Plant your roots in Christ and let him be the foundation for your life."*

- *It's the underpinning of a healthy family.* Proverbs 24:3 (TEV) says, *"Homes are built on the foundation of wisdom and understanding."* In a world that is constantly changing, strong families are based on God's unchanging truth.

- *It's the starting point of leadership.* You can never lead people farther than you've gone yourself. Proverbs 16:12b (MSG) says, *"Sound leadership has a moral foundation."*

- *It's the basis for your eternal reward in heaven.* Paul said, *"Whatever we build on that foundation will be tested by fire on the day of judgment . . . We will be rewarded if our building is left standing"* (1 Corinthians 3:12, 14 CEV).

- *God's truth is the only foundation that will last.* The Bible tells us that *"the sound, wholesome teachings of the Lord Jesus Christ . . . are the foundation for a godly life"* (1 Timothy 6:3 NLT), and that *"God's truth stands firm like a foundation stone . . . "* (2 Timothy 2:19 NLT).

Jesus concluded his Sermon on the Mount with a story illustrating this important truth. Two houses were built on different foundations. The house built on sand was destroyed when rain, floods, and wind swept it away. But the house built on the foundation of solid rock remained firm. He concluded, *"Therefore everyone who hears these words of mine and puts them into practice is like a wise man who built his house on the rock"* (Matthew 7:24 NIV). *The Message* paraphrase of this verse shows how important this is: *"These words I speak to you are not incidental additions to your life . . . They are foundational words, words to build a life on."*

I cannot recommend this curriculum more highly to you. It has changed our church, our staff, and thousands of lives. For too long, too many have thought of theology as something that doesn't relate to our everyday lives, but *Foundations* explodes that mold. This study makes it clear that the foundation of what we do and say in each day of our lives is what we believe. I am thrilled that this in-depth, life-changing curriculum is now being made available for everyone to use.

— Rick Warren, author of *The Purpose Driven® Life*

## PREFACE

Get ready for a radical statement, a pronouncement sure to make you wonder if we've lost our grip on reality: *There is nothing more exciting than doctrine!*

Track with us for a second on this. Doctrine is the study of what God has to say. What God has to say is always the truth. The truth gives me the right perspective on myself and on the world around me. The right perspective results in decisions of faith and experiences of joy. *That* is exciting!

The objective of *Foundations* is to present the basic truths of the Christian faith in a simple, systematic, and life-changing way—in other words, to teach doctrine. The question is, why? In a world in which people's lives are filled with crying needs, why teach doctrine? Because biblical doctrine has the answer to many of those crying needs! Please don't see this as a clash between needs-oriented and doctrine-oriented teaching. The truth is we need both. We all need to learn how to deal with worry in our lives. One of the keys to dealing with worry is an understanding of the biblical doctrine of the hope of heaven. Couples need to know what the Bible says about how to have a better marriage. They also need a deeper understanding of the doctrine of the Fatherhood of God, giving the assurance of God's love upon which all healthy relationships are built. Parents need to understand the Bible's practical insights for raising kids. They also need an understanding of the sovereignty of God, a certainty of the fact that God is in control, that will carry them through the inevitable ups and downs of being a parent. Doctrinal truth meets our deepest needs.

Welcome to a study that will have a lifelong impact on the way you look at everything around you and above you and within you. Helping you develop a "Christian worldview" is our goal as the writers of this study. A Christian worldview is the ability to see everything through the filter of God's truth. The time you dedicate to this study will lay a foundation for new perspectives that will have tremendous benefits for the rest of your life. This study will help you:

- Lessen the stress in everyday life

- See the real potential for growth the Lord has given you

- Increase your sense of security in an often troubling world

- Find new tools for helping others (your friends, your family, your children) find the right perspective on life

- Fall more deeply in love with the Lord

Throughout this study you'll see three types of sidebar sections designed to help you connect with the truths God tells us about himself, ourselves, and this world.

- *A Closer Look:* We'll take time to expand on a truth or look at it from a different perspective.

- *Key Personal Perspective:* The truth of doctrine always has a profound impact on our lives. In this section we'll focus on that personal impact.

- *Living on Purpose:* James 1:22 (NCV) says, *"Do what God's teaching says; when you only listen and do nothing, you are fooling yourselves."* In his book, *The Purpose Driven Life,* Rick Warren identifies God's five purposes for our lives. They are worship, fellowship, discipleship, ministry, and evangelism. We will focus on one of these five purposes in each lesson, and discuss how it relates to the subject of the study. This section is very important, so please be sure to leave time for it.

### Here is a brief explanation of the other features of this study guide.

*Looking Ahead/Catching Up:* You will open each meeting with an opportunity for everyone to check in with each other about how you are doing with the weekly assignments. Accountability is a key to success in this study!

*Key Verse:*  Each week you will find a key verse or Scripture passage for your group to read together. If someone in the group has a different translation, ask them to read it aloud so the group can get a bigger picture of the meaning of the passage.

*Video Lesson:*  There is a video lesson segment for the group to watch together each week. Take notes in the lesson outlines as you watch the video, and be sure to refer back to these notes during your discussion time.

*Discovery Questions:*  Each video segment is complemented by questions for group discussion. Please don't feel pressured to discuss every single question. The material in this study is meant to be your servant, not your master, so there is no reason to rush through the answers. Give everyone ample opportunity to share their thoughts. If you don't get through all of the discovery questions, that's okay.

*Prayer Direction:*  At the end of each session you will find suggestions for your group prayer time. Praying together is one of the greatest privileges of small group life. Please don't take it for granted.

Get ready for God to do incredible things in your life as you begin the adventure of learning more deeply about the most exciting message in the world: the truth about God!

— Tom Holladay and Kay Warren

# How to Use This Video Curriculum

Here is a brief explanation of the features on your small group DVD. These features include a *Group Lifter*, four *Video Teaching Sessions* by Tom Holladay and Kay Warren and a short video, *How to Become a Follower of Jesus Christ*, by Rick Warren. Here's how they work:

The *Group Lifter* is a brief video introduction by Tom Holladay giving you a sense of the objectives and purpose of this *Foundations* study on the Holy Spirit. Watch it together as a group at the beginning of your first session.

The *Video Teaching Sessions* provide you with the teaching for each week of the study. Watch these features with your group. After watching the video teaching session, continue in your study by working through the discussion questions and activities in the study guide.

Nothing is more important than the decision you make to accept Jesus Christ as your Lord and Savior. You will have the option to watch a short video presentation, *How to Become a Follower of Jesus Christ*, at the end of Session Three. In this brief video segment, Rick Warren explains the importance of having Christ as the Savior of your life and how you can become part of the family of God. If everyone in your group is already a follower of Christ, or if you feel there is a better time to play this segment, continue your session by turning to the Discovery Questions in your DVD study guide. You can also select this video presentation separately on the Main Menu of the DVD for viewing at any time.

*Follow these simple steps for a successful small group session:*

1. Hosts: Watch the video session and write down your answers to the discussion questions in the study guide before your group arrives.

2. Group: Open your group meeting by using the "Looking Ahead" or "Catching Up" section of your lesson.

3. Group: Watch the video teaching lesson and follow along in the outlines in the study guide.

4. Group: Complete the rest of the discussion materials for each session in the study guide.

It's just that simple. Have a great study together!

# Session One

# 1

# GOD, THE HOLY SPIRIT

## LOOKING AHEAD

1. What do you hope to get out of this small group study?

*New & greater understanding about His work in my life.*

2. What image comes to mind when you think of the Holy Spirit? Scripture tells us that when we accept Christ, the Holy Spirit comes to live inside us, yet he is probably the most difficult person of the Trinity to understand. Our ideas about the Holy Spirit may be influenced by many factors, such as upbringing, media, or personal experiences. *Unseen =*

Spend a few minutes describing your present concept of the Holy Spirit.

*A helper who walks beside Me - GPS for my life.*

**Key Verse**

*. . . let the Holy Spirit fill and control you.*

Ephesians 5:18b (NLT)

**BIBLE TEACHING**

Watch the video lesson now and take notes in your outline on pages 3–5.

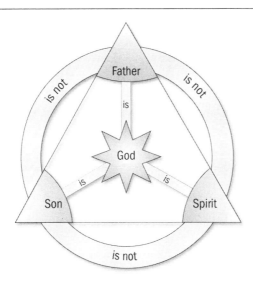

## TRUTHS ABOUT THE TRINITY

1. God relates to us as a Trinity, three persons in one being.

2. God is one; he is not three Gods, but one God (Deuteronomy 6:4).

3. The Father is God, the Son is God, and the Spirit is God.

4. The three are distinct from one another: separate, but one.

## Historical Background

In the Old Testament the Holy Spirit came upon people at
_various_ times for _specific_ purposes.
He never indwelt anyone _permantly_ .

---

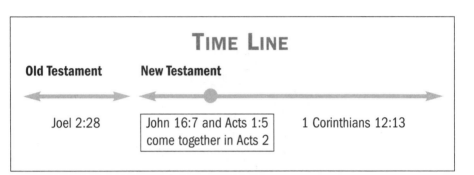

### TIME LINE

**Old Testament**    **New Testament**

Joel 2:28 | John 16:7 and Acts 1:5 come together in Acts 2 | 1 Corinthians 12:13

---

*"For John baptized with water, but in a few days you will be baptized with the Holy Spirit."* (Acts 1:5 NIV)

*For we were all baptized by one Spirit into one body—whether Jews or Greeks, slave or free—and we were all given the one Spirit to drink.* (1 Corinthians 12:13 NIV)

- Do we have to have an _experience_
  to be filled and empowered by the Holy Spirit? No

## What Is the Role of the Holy Spirit Today?

**The Holy Spirit** _Regenerates_ **me.**

- Definition: To give _Re - birth - born again_

> He saved us. It was not because of any good deeds that we
> ourselves had done, but because of his own mercy that he
> saved us, through the Holy Spirit, who gives us new birth and
> new life by washing us. (Titus 3:5 TEV)

- Before I came to Christ, I was _Spiritually dead_ .
- Now I am _Spiritually Alive_ through the new birth.

> "What gives life is God's Spirit; human power is of no use at
> all. The words I have spoken to you bring God's life-giving
> Spirit." (John 6:63 TEV)

## DISCOVERY QUESTIONS

1. How has the teaching you heard in this session helped you better
   understand the reality of the Holy Spirit? Has it helped you see him
   as God himself, rather than as a force or emotion of God? What
   difference does this truth make to you personally?

2. Look again at John 3:1–16. Why do you think it was so difficult for a religious man such as Nicodemus to understand spiritual rebirth? How do Jesus' words to him help you grasp what it means to be born of the Spirit?

Sometimes our religion keeps us from seeing what is truly spiritual. Religion has been called "man's attempt to reach to God." When our relationship with God is shielded by man-made rules and traditions, it is difficult to see what the Spirit is doing. Jesus encouraged Nicodemus to return to the simple truths, beginning with birth. He wants us all to realize that Christianity is God reaching out to man.

**Did You Get It?** How has this week's study helped you to see God's Spirit as a person with whom you have a relationship?

**Share with Someone:** Think of a person you can encourage with the truth you learned this week. Write their name in the space below.

*Worship*

During your personal prayer times this week, focus on thanking God for the good things he has done in your life. It's all too easy to focus on how far we have to go in our growth as believers. We need to balance that out by focusing on how far we have come. You are not yet all you should be as a Christian, but you are also not what you used to be!

Pay close attention this week to the Holy Spirit's work in you. Be ready to share any special insights with the group next time.

# PRAYER DIRECTION

Read together Psalm 51:10–12. Now, as a group, spend some time in prayer thanking God the Holy Spirit for his work in your life. Along with David, thank God for the Holy Spirit's presence in your life, making you a new creation. Let gratitude guide your prayers.

## NOTES

# Session two

# 2

## THE ROLE OF
## THE HOLY SPIRIT

## CATCHING UP

1. Who did you share last week's truth with? What did you learn by focusing on God's goodness during last week's "Living on Purpose" activity?

2. Did you notice that you were more aware of the Holy Spirit's presence in your life as a result of last week's lesson? Share any opportunities or insights you may have observed.

### Key Verse

*For we were all baptized by one Spirit into one body—whether Jews or Greeks, slave or free—and we were all given the one Spirit to drink.*

1 Corinthians 12:13 (NIV)

**BIBLE TEACHING**
Watch the video lesson now and take notes in your outline on pages 11–13.

## The Role of the Holy Spirit Today

### *The Holy Spirit* _____ **me.**

1. The baptism of the Holy Spirit is the placing of the Christian into the _____ and into _____ .

   > *For we were all baptized by one Spirit into one body—whether Jews or Greeks, slave or free—and we were all given the one Spirit to drink.* (1 Corinthians 12:13 NIV)

2. The baptism of the Holy Spirit is a _____ occurring at the moment of salvation.

3. The baptism of the Holy Spirit is a _____ for all believers.

   > [26]*You are all sons of God through faith in Christ Jesus,* [27]*for all of you who were baptized into Christ have clothed yourselves with Christ.* (Galatians 3:26–27 NIV)

The baptism of the Holy Spirit is a universal gift to believers. Nowhere in the Bible are Christians instructed to desire or seek the baptism of the Holy Spirit. We should not pray for it, seek it, or try to achieve it. We already have it.

**Note:** Much of the confusion over the baptism of the Holy Spirit comes about because of the failure to make a distinction between the baptism of the Holy Spirit and the filling of the Holy Spirit. The baptism of the Holy Spirit is something God does for us in establishing our relationship with Jesus Christ. The filling of the Holy Spirit is the daily experience of our yielding to the Holy Spirit's control. We will discuss the filling of the Holy Spirit in detail in the next session.

*The Holy Spirit* _____ **me.**

> *Do you not know that your body is a temple of the Holy Spirit,*
> *who is in you, whom you have received from God? . . .*
> (1 Corinthians 6:19 NIV)

*The Holy Spirit* _____ **me.**

> *And you also were included in Christ when you heard the*
> *word of truth, the gospel of your salvation. Having believed,*
> *you were marked in him with a seal, the promised Holy Spirit.*
> (Ephesians 1:13 NIV)

- Sealing implies _____ and _____ .

*The Holy Spirit is the* _____ .

> *. . . who is a deposit guaranteeing our inheritance until the*
> *redemption of those who are God's possession—to the praise*
> *of his glory.* (Ephesians 1:14 NIV)

> *Now it is God who has made us for this very purpose and has*
> *given us the Spirit as a deposit, guaranteeing what is to come.*
> (2 Corinthians 5:5 NIV)

---

**KEY PERSONAL PERSPECTIVE**

*Putting Knowledge into Action*

1. You may have realized that you have never been born again; you have never experienced the regeneration of the Holy Spirit. Come to God, repent of living life to please yourself, and ask him to give you a new birth and eternal life with him.

2. You may have been confused about the baptism of the Holy Spirit. You've prayed and sought another experience with God that would change you forever. Now you see that the miraculous has already happened to you. Thank God for putting you in Christ where you belong with all in God's family. Thank him that his work is so powerful and complete that you never have to repeat it. Thank God that because you are in Christ, he now sees you covered by Jesus' righteousness. You are pure, spotless, and holy before him.

3. Thank God that his promises are faithful and that his pledge to keep you forever is true. Thank the Holy Spirit for sealing you so that you are safe from losing your salvation. Spend a few moments thinking of the time when you will receive all that has been promised to you; when God's engagement ring becomes a wedding ring, and you will sit with him at the Marriage Supper of the Lamb in heaven.

---

## DISCOVERY QUESTIONS

1. First Corinthians 12:13 and Galatians 3:26–27 indicate that all believers are baptized in the Holy Spirit. What does it mean for you that you are "totally immersed" in the Spirit of God? How does it affect your perspective on other believers when you realize that we are ALL baptized—"totally immersed"—in the Spirit of God?

2. The knowledge that we are sealed by the Holy Spirit is a tremendous source of security in our lives as believers. What is one place in your life you regularly need to draw upon that "account" for your security?

**Did You Get It?** How has this week's study helped you see the importance of the fact that you are baptized, indwelt, and sealed by God's Spirit?

**Share with Someone:** Think of a person you can encourage with the truth you learned this week. Write their name in the space below.

---

## LIVING ON PURPOSE
### *Discipleship*

Being a believer in Christ does not mean living the Christian life on our own power. We must rely on the daily power that comes from a fresh filling of the Holy Spirit. There is likely nothing more important you could do for one another as a group than to be aware of and to pray for one another's needs in this all-important area. What one thing could you do to be more consistently filled with the Spirit? Take a few minutes at the conclusion of your small group time to make a list of each person's answer to that question. If possible, copy the list on a 3 x 5 card for each person in your group so you can all pray for each other. The list would look something like this:

Specific prayer requests for my group—for each person's "one thing" to be more consistently filled with God's Spirit:

John: A daily quiet time

Mary: Trusting in God's forgiveness

Bill: Thinking about God at the beginning of each hour

Ellen: Taking the time to pray for my family

Steve: Choosing to say "yes" to God

Jan: Seeing the people at my work as people Jesus loves

End the study by praying for each other that the work of God the Father, God the Son, and God the Spirit will be both personal and powerful in your everyday lives.

## PRAYER DIRECTION

Take some time as a group to talk about your specific prayer requests and to pray for one another.

## NOTES

# 3

Session three

## THE FILLING OF
## THE HOLY SPIRIT

## CATCHING UP

1. What did you learn about daily fillings with the Holy Spirit during the past week?

2. If you could pick one place in your life where you would like to see God working in greater ways, where would it be?

### Key Verse

*But the spiritual man has insight into everything, and that bothers and baffles the man of the world, who can't understand him at all.*

1 Corinthians 2:15 (LB)

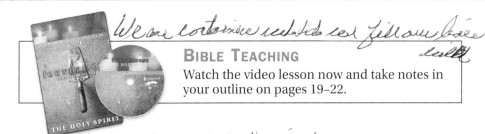

# the filling of THE HOLY SPIRIT

*We are continue until did we fill our base will*

**BIBLE TEACHING**
Watch the video lesson now and take notes in your outline on pages 19–22.

*What feel is to be how the H S in for us—*

## Our Need for the Filling of the Holy Spirit

The Bible says that everyone is in one of three spiritual positions:[1]

### 1. The _____human Natural_____ man

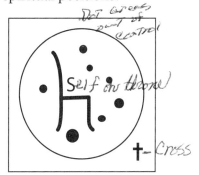

[1]*As for you, you were dead in your transgressions and sins, [2]in which you used to live when you followed the ways of this world and of the ruler of the kingdom of the air, the spirit who is now at work in those who are disobedient.* (Ephesians 2:1–2 NIV)

*But the man who isn't a Christian can't understand and can't accept these thoughts from God, which the Holy Spirit teaches us. They sound foolish to him because only those who have the Holy Spirit within them can understand what the Holy Spirit means. Others just can't take it in.* (1 Corinthians 2:14 LB)

### 2. The _____Spiritual_____ *opposite of natural* man

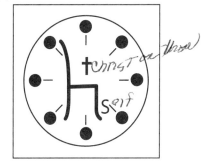

*But the spiritual man has insight into everything, and that bothers and baffles the man of the world, who can't understand him at all.* (1 Corinthians 2:15 LB)

*Not perfect*

---

[1]The following three illustrations are taken from *Have You Made the Wonderful Discovery of the Spirit-Filled Life?* (Bill Bright, Orlando, Fla.: New Life Publications, 1990), used by permission of Campus Crusade for Christ.

3. The ___Carnal Self___ man *back on* *the one*

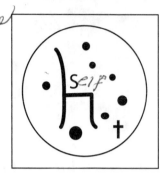

> ¹Brothers, I could not address you as spiritual but as worldly—mere infants in Christ. ²I gave you milk, not solid food, for you were not yet ready for it. Indeed, you are still not ready. ³You are still worldly. For since there is jealousy and quarreling among you, are you not worldly? Are you not acting like mere men? (1 Corinthians 3:1–3 NIV)

*Romans 7* *I in sins*

*Romans 8 the HS is mentioned method of*

## What Is the Filling of the Holy Spirit?

> ¹⁸Do not get drunk on wine, which leads to debauchery. Instead, be filled with the Spirit. ¹⁹Speak to one another with psalms, hymns and spiritual songs. Sing and make music in your heart to the Lord, ²⁰always giving thanks to God the Father for everything, in the name of our Lord Jesus Christ. ²¹Submit to one another out of reverence for Christ. (Ephesians 5:18–21 NIV)

### Four Truths from Ephesians 5:18–21

1. The verb used for "filled" is plural, implying ___ALL___ are to be filled.

2. The verb used for "filled" is present tense (be filled), implying ___Repeated Action___ . ___like Breathing —___

3. The verb used for "filled" is passive, implying the filling is something done ___to you — God works in me,___

   *Release control to God — spong in water.*

4. The verb used for "filled" is imperative, implying _____

   *Command — be filled all the time not just some of the time)*

# tHe fiLLiNG of THE HOLY SPIRIT

---

## A CLOSER LOOK
### What's the Difference?

| Baptism of the Holy Spirit | Filling of the Holy Spirit |
| --- | --- |
| A positional* truth | An experiential* truth |
| Not commanded | Commanded |
| A one-time event | A continuous event |
| Puts believer in the position to receive power | Power itself |

*Positional truth is who we are because of our faith in Christ. Experiential truth is how we are to live based on that position. One is a root, the other is a fruit.

---

## Signs of the Filling of the Holy Spirit

There is often confusion over "signs" that indicate the Holy Spirit has filled someone.

### 1. Personal experiences that may or may not accompany filling:

*Emotionalism* _____ : emotion or feeling is not necessarily part of being filled.

• *Exceptional* _____ ability: God works within the framework of our limitations and natural abilities.

• Personal _Charisma_ _____: may be mistaken for filling.

• *Tranquility* _____ of mind and spirit: great Spirit-filled believers have experienced frustrations, discouragement, and disappointments.

• Speaking in _Tongues_ _____ (Acts 2, Acts 9): throughout history, some Christians speak in tongues when filled, others do not.

## 2. False teachings concerning what must accompany filling:

- *freedom* from problems: filling doesn't make all problems disappear, but it does give us the strength and wisdom to better face our problems.

- Total freedom from *Temptation* : Jesus faced one of the greatest times of temptation immediately after the Spirit came upon him following his baptism. Some who are filled experience more temptation than when not filled.

- Sinless *perfection* : Obviously this is not true! Every Christian sins and must trust in God's forgiveness and ask for renewed filling every day.

## 3. Biblical and universal signs of filling:

- The *gift* of the Spirit

   *A spiritual gift is given to each of us as a means of helping the entire church.* (1 Corinthians 12:7 NLT)

- The *fruit* of the Spirit

   *But the fruit of the Spirit is love, joy, peace, patience, kindness, goodness, faithfulness, gentleness and self-control.* (Galatians 5:22–23 NIV)

- The *power* of the Spirit (Acts 1:8; Ephesians 3:20; Acts 4:29)

   *". . . my power works best in your weakness . . ."* (2 Corinthians 12:9 NLT)

# the fiLLinG of THE HOLY SPIRIT

### "How to Become a Follower of Jesus Christ"

Have you ever surrendered your life to Jesus Christ? Take a few minutes with your group to watch a brief video by Pastor Rick Warren on how to become part of the family of God. It is included on the Main Menu of this DVD.

*ADMIT - Believe - Confess Recieve - Inviting him To Be Lord of my Life. CEO*

## DISCOVERY QUESTIONS

1. Was there ever a time when you were closer to God than you are right now? Can you remember what it was like? What happened to change that closeness? If you are presently as close to God as you've ever been, what has brought about that closeness?

2. It has been said that up to 95 percent of believers are living worldly lives—lives characterized by some of those struggles we talked about in this session. Why do you believe it is so easy and common to settle for less than God's best in our spiritual lives?

**Did You Get It?** How has this week's study helped you understand the difference between the baptism of the Spirit and the filling of the Spirit? The real test of that understanding is being able to explain it to someone else.

**Share with Someone:** Think of a person you can encourage with the truth you learned this week. Write their name in the space below.

## LIVING ON PURPOSE
### Fellowship

Paul reminds us:

> You show that you are a letter from Christ . . . written not with ink but with the Spirit of the living God, not on tablets of stone but on tablets of human hearts. (2 Corinthians 3:3 NIV)

How do you see God "writing on the hearts" of your group? Take some time to make this a personal expression of encouragement. Go around the circle in your group and share with each person, one at a time, "This is one way I see God's Spirit in your life." At least two or three should share with each person. This may feel a little uncomfortable at first, but if we cheer someone for hitting a home run or applaud a promotion at work, how much more important is it to recognize God's work in the lives of others?

## PRAYER DIRECTION

Take a few minutes to express your praise to God for the work the Holy Spirit is doing in you. Praise him, corporately, for his guiding hand upon you and within you, keeping you from living a life based on pointless pursuits.

Session four

# 4

BEING FILLED WITH
THE HOLY SPIRIT

## CATCHING UP

1. What did you learn about seeing God's Spirit at work in others during last week's "Living on Purpose" activity?

2. If someone observed your group over the past few weeks, how would they complete the following sentence? "When I look at your group, I see . . ."

**Key Verse**

*. . . the mind controlled by the Spirit is life and peace.*

Romans 8:6 (NIV)

**BIBLE TEACHING**

Watch the video lesson now and take notes in your outline on pages 27–28.

> [16]*"And I will ask the Father, and he will give you another Counselor to be with you forever—*[17]*the Spirit of truth. The world cannot accept him, because it neither sees him nor knows him. But you know him, for he lives with you and will be in you."* (John 14:16–17 NIV)

## How to Be Filled with the Holy Spirit
## (or How Can I Be Filled with the Holy Spirit?)

1. _____*Recognize your thirst* for filling and desire it._

> [37]*On the last and greatest day of the Feast, Jesus stood and said in a loud voice, "If anyone is thirsty, let him come to me and drink.* [38]*Whoever believes in me, as the Scripture has said, streams of living water will flow from within him."* [39]*By this he meant the Spirit, whom those who believed in him were later to receive. Up to that time the Spirit had not been given, since Jesus had not yet been glorified.* (John 7:37–39 NIV)

2. *Repent* _____ *sins and receive God's cleansing.*

> *But if we confess our sins to him, he can be depended on to forgive us and to cleanse us from every wrong. And it is perfectly proper for God to do this for us because Christ died to wash away our sins.* (1 John 1:9 LB)

> *"My people have committed two sins: They have forsaken me, the spring of living water, and have dug their own cisterns, broken cisterns that cannot hold water."* (Jeremiah 2:13 NIV)

3. _Yeald all of yourself_ **to the Holy Spirit's control.**

- Let Jesus _be Lord_ daily.

  *I have been crucified with Christ and I no longer live, but Christ lives in me. The life I live in the body, I live by faith in the Son of God, who loved me and gave himself for me.* (Galatians 2:20 NIV)

- _Deny ourselves_ daily.

  *[34]Then he called the crowd to him along with his disciples and said: "If anyone would come after me, he must deny himself and take up his cross and follow me. [35]For whoever wants to save his life will lose it, but whoever loses his life for me and for the gospel will save it."* (Mark 8:34–35 NIV)

4. _Trust God_ **to fill you as he said he would.**

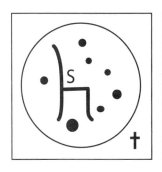 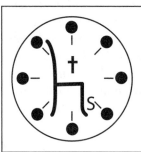 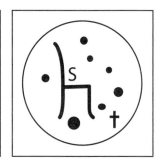

## DISCOVERY QUESTIONS

1. As you now understand it, what is the difference between the baptism of the Holy Spirit and the filling of the Holy Spirit? From the first session, how has your picture of the Holy Spirit changed as a result of this series? How can you be filled every day? What difference might you expect the filling of the Spirit to make in your life?

2. Look back at the three circles on page 28 that describe the three spiritual positions. Which circle represents your life at this moment? If Jesus is not Lord in every area of your life, what will it take for you to give him the throne of your life?

3. Where do you find yourself "digging your own wells," as discussed in this study?

4. Where do you need to trust God for the power to do what he is leading you to do? In what area of your life do you need to act in faith?

5. You've spent the last few weeks together studying and discussing the Holy Spirit. As you end this study, take time to complete one of these statements:

One thing I've really appreciated about doing this study with this group is . . .

One way this group has helped me better understand the Holy Spirit is . . .

When I think back on this study, one thing I won't forget is . . .

**Did You Get It?** How has this week's study helped you to see that the filling of the Holy Spirit is something you need every day?

**Share with Someone:** Has anyone had an opportunity to share the principle of the Spirit-filled life with a relative, friend, neighbor, or co-worker during this study? If so, what happened? As a group, encourage each other to continue to look for opportunities to share this principle with those who may struggle to live the Spirit-filled life on a daily basis.

---

### LIVING ON PURPOSE

#### Worship

The Bible says that one sign of the Spirit filling our lives is seen when we sing songs of worship together.

> [18]. . . *let the Holy Spirit fill and control you.* [19]*Then you will sing psalms and hymns and spiritual songs among yourselves, making music to the Lord in your hearts.* [20]*And you will always give thanks for everything to God the Father in the name of our Lord Jesus Christ.* (Ephesians 5:18-20 NLT)

Even if your group isn't used to singing together, stretch out of your comfort zones by singing some worship songs together to close this meeting. If no one plays an instrument, you could put in a worship CD and sing along. If you're nervous about doing this, turn the music up!

---

## PRAYER DIRECTION

Take some time as a group to talk about your specific prayer requests and to pray for one another. Thank God for this series, and for helping you gain a clearer understanding of the Holy Spirit. Express your gratitude for his presence in your lives.

## NOTES

appendix

# Appendix

## Theology of the Trinity

| | |
|---|---|
| *Introduction* | The word *Trinity* is never used, nor is the doctrine of Trinitarianism ever explicitly taught, in the Scriptures, but Trinitarianism is the best explication [detailed explanation] of the biblical evidence. It is a crucial doctrine for Christianity because it focuses on who God is, and particularly on the deity of Jesus Christ. Because Trinitarianism is not taught explicitly in the Scriptures, the study of the doctrine is an exercise in putting together biblical themes and data through a systematic theological study and through looking at the historical development of the present orthodox view of what the biblical presentation of the Trinity is. |
| *Essential Elements of the Trinity* | God is One.<br><br>Each of the persons within the Godhead is Deity.<br><br>The oneness of God and the threeness of God are not contradictory.<br><br>The Trinity (Father, Son, and Holy Spirit) is eternal.<br><br>Each of the persons of God is of the same essence and is not inferior or superior to the others in essence.<br><br>The Trinity is a mystery which we will never be able to understand fully. |

| *Biblical Teaching* | *Old Testament* | *New Testament* |
|---|---|---|
| *God Is One* | "Hear, O Israel: The LORD our God, the LORD is one." (Deuteronomy 6:4; cf. 20:2–4) | "Now to the King eternal, immortal, invisible, the only God, be honor and glory for ever and ever. Amen." (1 Timothy 1:17; cf. 1 Corinthians 8:4–6; 1 Timothy 2:5–6; James 2:19) |

| Biblical Teaching | Old Testament | New Testament |
|---|---|---|
| *Three Distinct Persons as Deity* | **The Father:** "He said to me, 'You are my Son; today I have become your Father.'" (Psalm 2:7) | "... who have been chosen according to the foreknowledge of God the Father." (1 Peter 1:2; cf. John 1:17–18; 1 Corinthians 8:6; Philippians 2:11) |
| | **The Son:** "He said to me, 'You are my Son; today I have become your Father.'" (Psalm 2:7; cf. Hebrews 1:1–13; Psalm 68:18; Isaiah 6:1–3; 9:6) | "As soon as Jesus was baptized, he went up out of the water. At that moment heaven was opened, and he saw the Spirit of God descending like a dove and lighting on him. And a voice from heaven said, 'This is my Son, whom I love; with him I am well pleased.'" (Matthew 3:16–17) |
| | **The Holy Spirit:** "In the beginning God created the heavens and the earth ... and the Spirit of God was hovering over the waters." (Genesis 1:1–2; cf. Exodus 31:3; Judges 15:14; Isaiah 11:2) | "Then Peter said, 'Ananias, how is it that Satan has so filled your heart that you have lied to the Holy Spirit ... ? You have not lied to men but to God.'" (Acts 5:3–4; cf. 2 Corinthians 3:17) |
| *Plurality of Persons in the Godhead* | The use of plural pronouns points to, or at least suggests, the plurality of persons within the Godhead in the Old Testament. "Then God said, 'Let us make man in our image, in our likeness ... ' " (Genesis 1:26) | The use of the singular word "name" when referring to God the Father, Son, and Holy Spirit indicates a unity within the threeness of God. "Therefore go and make disciples of all nations, baptizing them in the name of the Father and of the Son and of the Holy Spirit." (Matthew 28:19) |

| | Attribute | Father | Son | Holy Spirit |
|---|---|---|---|---|
| **Persons of the Same Essence:** *Attributes Applied to Each Person* | **Eternality** | Psalm 90:2 | John 1:2; Revelation 1:8, 17 | Hebrews 9:14 |
| | **Power** | 1 Peter 1:5 | 2 Corinthians 12:9 | Romans 15:19 |
| | **Omniscience** | Jeremiah 17:10 | Revelation 2:23 | 1 Corinthians 2:11 |
| | **Omnipresence** | Jeremiah 23:24 | Matthew 18:20 | Psalm 139:7 |
| | **Holiness** | Revelation 15:4 | Acts 3:14 | Acts 1:8 |
| | **Truth** | John 7:28 | Revelation 3:7 | 1 John 5:6 |
| | **Benevolence** | Romans 2:4 | Ephesians 5:25 | Nehemiah 9:20 |
| **Equality with Different Roles:** *Activities Involving* | **Creation of Man** | Genesis 2:7 | Colossians 1:16 | Genesis 1:2; Job 26:13 |
| | **Creation of the World** | Psalm 102:25 | Colossians 1:16 | Job 33:4 |
| | **Baptism of Christ** | Matthew 3:17 | Matthew 3:16–17 | Matthew 3:16 |
| | **Death of Christ** | Hebrews 9:14 | Hebrews 9:14 | Hebrews 9:14 |

Source: Taken from *Charts of Christian Theology and Doctrine* by H. Wayne House. Copyright © 1992 by H. Wayne House. Used by permission of Zondervan.

# Small Group Resources

## HELPS FOR HOSTS

### Top Ten Ideas for New Hosts

Congratulations! As the host of your small group, you have responded to the call to help shepherd Jesus' flock. Few other tasks in the family of God surpass the contribution you will be making.

As you prepare to facilitate your group, whether it is one session or the entire series, here are a few thoughts to keep in mind. We encourage you to read and review these tips with each new discussion host before he or she leads.

Remember you are not alone. God knows everything about you, and he knew you would be asked to facilitate your group. Even though you may not feel ready, this is common for all good hosts. God promises, *"I will never leave you; I will never abandon you"* (Hebrews 13:5 TEV). Whether you are facilitating for one evening, several weeks, or a lifetime, you will be blessed as you serve.

1. **Don't try to do it alone.** Pray right now for God to help you build a healthy team. If you can enlist a cohost to help you shepherd the group, you will find your experience much richer. This is your chance to involve as many people as you can in building a healthy group. All you have to do is ask people to help. You'll be surprised at the response.

2. **Be friendly and be yourself.** God wants to use your unique gifts and temperament. Be sure to greet people at the door with a big smile . . . this can set the mood for the whole gathering. Remember, they are taking as big a step to show up at your house as you are to lead this group! Don't try to do things exactly like another host; do them in a way that fits you. Admit when you don't have an answer and apologize when you make a mistake. Your group will love you for it and you'll sleep better at night.

3. **Prepare for your meeting ahead of time.** Review the session and write down your responses to each question. Pay special attention to exercises that ask group members to do something other than engage in discussion. These exercises will help your group live what the Bible teaches, not just talk about it. Be sure you understand how an exercise works. If the exercise employs one of the items in the Small Group Resources section (such as the Group Guidelines), be sure to look over that item so you'll know how it works.

4. **Pray for your group members by name.** Before you begin your session, take a few moments and pray for each member by name. You may want to review the prayer list at least once a week. Ask God to use your time together to touch the heart of every person in your group. Expect God to lead you to whomever he wants you to encourage or challenge in a special way. If you listen, God will surely lead.

5. **When you ask a question, be patient.** Someone will eventually respond. Sometimes people need a moment or two of silence to think about the question. If silence doesn't bother you, it won't bother anyone else. After someone responds, affirm the response with a simple "thanks" or "great answer." Then ask, "How about somebody else?" or "Would someone who hasn't shared like to add anything?" Be sensitive to new people or reluctant members who aren't ready to say, pray, or do anything. If you give them a safe setting, they will blossom over time. If someone in your group is a "wallflower" who sits silently through every session, consider talking to them privately and encouraging them to participate. Let them know how important they are to you—that they are loved and appreciated—and that the group would value their input. Remember, still water often runs deep.

6. **Provide transitions between questions.** Ask if anyone would like to read the paragraph or Bible passage. Don't call on anyone, but ask for a volunteer, and then be patient until someone begins. Be sure to thank the person who reads aloud.

7. **Break into smaller groups occasionally.** With a greater opportunity to talk in a small circle, people will connect more with the study, apply more quickly what they're learning, and ultimately get more out of their small group experience. A small circle also encourages a quiet person to participate and tends to minimize the effects of a more vocal or dominant member.

8. **Small circles are also helpful during prayer time.** People who are unaccustomed to praying aloud will feel more comfortable trying it with just two or three others. Also, prayer requests won't take as much time, so circles will have more time to actually pray. When you gather back with the whole group, you can have one person from each circle briefly update everyone on the prayer requests from their subgroups. The other great aspect of subgrouping is that it fosters leadership development. As you ask people in the group to facilitate discussion or to lead a prayer circle, it gives them a small leadership step that can build their confidence.

9. **Rotate facilitators occasionally.** You may be perfectly capable of hosting each time, but you will help others grow in their faith and gifts if you give them opportunities to host the group.

10. **One final challenge (for new or first-time hosts).** Before your first opportunity to lead, look up each of the six passages that follow. Read each one as a devotional exercise to help prepare you with a shepherd's heart. Trust us on this one. If you do this, you will be more than ready for your first meeting.

### Matthew 9:36–38 (NIV)

*36When Jesus saw the crowds, he had compassion on them, because they were harassed and helpless, like sheep without a shepherd. 37Then he said to his disciples, "The harvest is plentiful but the workers are few. 38Ask the Lord of the harvest, therefore, to send out workers into his harvest field."*

### John 10:14–15 (NIV)

*14I am the good shepherd; I know my sheep and my sheep know me—15just as the Father knows me and I know the Father—and I lay down my life for the sheep.*

## 1 Peter 5:2-4 (NIV)

*²Be shepherds of God's flock that is under your care, serving as overseers—not because you must, but because you are willing, as God wants you to be; ³not greedy for money, but eager to serve; not lording it over those entrusted to you, but being examples to the flock. ⁴And when the Chief Shepherd appears, you will receive the crown of glory that will never fade away.*

## Philippians 2:1-5 (NIV)

*¹If you have any encouragement from being united with Christ, if any comfort from his love, if any fellowship with the Spirit, if any tenderness and compassion, ²then make my joy complete by being like-minded, having the same love, being one in spirit and purpose. ³Do nothing out of selfish ambition or vain conceit, but in humility consider others better than yourselves. ⁴Each of you should look not only to your own interests, but also to the interests of others. ⁵Your attitude should be the same as that of Jesus Christ.*

## Hebrews 10:23-25 (NIV)

*²³Let us hold unswervingly to the hope we profess, for he who promised is faithful. ²⁴And let us consider how we may spur one another on toward love and good deeds. ²⁵Let us not give up meeting together, as some are in the habit of doing, but let us encourage one another—and all the more as you see the Day approaching.*

## 1 Thessalonians 2:7-8, 11-12 (NIV)

*⁷. . . but we were gentle among you, like a mother caring for her little children. ⁸We loved you so much that we were delighted to share with you not only the gospel of God but our lives as well, because you had become so dear to us. . . . ¹¹For you know that we dealt with each of you as a father deals with his own children, ¹²encouraging, comforting and urging you to live lives worthy of God, who calls you into his kingdom and glory.*

# FREQUENTLY ASKED QUESTIONS

### How long will this group meet?

This volume of *Foundations: Holy Spirit* is four sessions long. We encourage your group to add a fifth session for a celebration. In your final session, each group member may decide if he or she desires to continue on for another study. At that time you may also want to do some informal evaluation, discuss your Group Guidelines, and decide which study you want to do next. We recommend you visit our website at **www.saddlebackresources.com** for more video-based small group studies.

### Who is the host?

The host is the person who coordinates and facilitates your group meetings. In addition to a host, we encourage you to select one or more group members to lead your group discussions. Several other responsibilities can be rotated, including refreshments, prayer requests, worship, or keeping up with those who miss a meeting. Shared ownership in the group helps everybody grow.

### Where do we find new group members?

Recruiting new members can be a challenge for groups, especially new groups with just a few people, or existing groups that lose a few people along the way. We encourage you to use the *Circles of Life* diagram on page 46 of this DVD study guide to brainstorm a list of people from your workplace, church, school, neighborhood, family, and so on. Then pray for the people on each member's list. Allow each member to invite several people from their list. Some groups fear that newcomers will interrupt the intimacy that members have built over time. However, groups that welcome newcomers generally gain strength with the infusion of new blood. Remember, the next person you add just might become a friend for eternity. Logistically, groups find different ways to add members. Some groups remain permanently open, while others choose to open periodically, such as at the beginning or end of a study. If your group becomes too large for easy, face-to-face conversations, you can subgroup, forming a second discussion group in another room.

### How do we handle the child care needs in our group?

Child care needs must be handled very carefully. This is a sensitive issue. We suggest you seek creative solutions as a group. One common solution is to have the adults meet in the living room and share the cost of a babysitter (or two) who can be with the kids in another part of the house. Another popular option is to have one home for the kids and a second home (close by) for the adults. If desired, the adults could rotate the responsibility of providing a lesson for the kids. This last option is great with school-age kids and can be a huge blessing to families.

## GROUP GUIDELINES

It's a good idea for every group to put words to their shared values, expectations, and commitments. Such guidelines will help you avoid unspoken agendas and unmet expectations. We recommend you discuss your guidelines during Session One in order to lay the foundation for a healthy group experience. Feel free to modify anything that does not work for your group.

### *We agree to the following values:*

**Clear Purpose**
To grow healthy spiritual lives by building a healthy small group community

**Group Attendance**
To give priority to the group meeting (call if I am absent or late)

**Safe Environment**
To create a safe place where people can be heard and feel loved (no quick answers, snap judgments, or simple fixes)

**Be Confidential**
To keep anything that is shared strictly confidential and within the group

**Conflict Resolution**
To avoid gossip and to immediately resolve any concerns by following the principles of Matthew 18:15–17

**Spiritual Health**
To give group members permission to speak into my life and help me live a healthy, balanced spiritual life that is pleasing to God

**Limit Our Freedom**
To limit our freedom by not serving or consuming alcohol during small group meetings or events so as to avoid causing a weaker brother or sister to stumble (1 Corinthians 8:1–13; Romans 14:19–21)

**Welcome Newcomers**   To invite friends who might benefit from this study and warmly welcome newcomers

**Building Relationships**   To get to know the other members of the group and pray for them regularly

**Other**   _____

*We have also discussed and agreed on the following items:*

**Child Care**

_____

_____

**Starting Time**

_____

**Ending Time**

_____

If you haven't already done so, take a few minutes to fill out the *Small Group Calendar* on page 50.

## CIRCLES OF LIFE—SMALL GROUP CONNECTIONS

### Discover who you can connect in community

Use this chart to help carry out one of the values in the Group Guidelines, to "Welcome Newcomers."

*"Follow me, and I will make you fishers of men."* (Matthew 4:19 KJV)

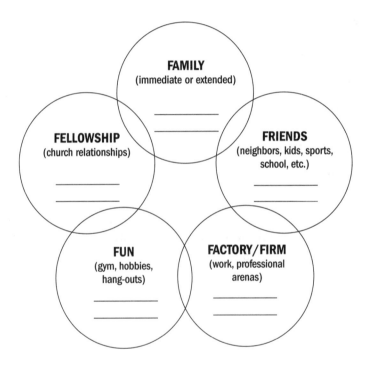

*Follow this simple three-step process:*

1. List 1–2 people in each circle.

2. Prayerfully select one person or couple from your list and tell your group about them.

3. Give them a call and invite them to your next meeting. Over 50 percent of those invited to a small group say, "Yes!"

## SMALL GROUP PRAYER AND PRAISE REPORT

This is a place where you can write each other's requests for prayer. You can also make a note when God answers a prayer. Pray for each other's requests. If you're new to group prayer, it's okay to pray silently or to pray by using just one sentence: "God, please help

_____ to _____ . "

| DATE | PERSON | PRAYER REQUEST | PRAISE REPORT |
|------|--------|----------------|---------------|
|      |        |                |               |
|      |        |                |               |
|      |        |                |               |
|      |        |                |               |
|      |        |                |               |
|      |        |                |               |
|      |        |                |               |
|      |        |                |               |
|      |        |                |               |
|      |        |                |               |

## SMALL GROUP PRAYER AND PRAISE REPORT

| DATE | PERSON | PRAYER REQUEST | PRAISE REPORT |
|------|--------|----------------|---------------|
|      |        |                |               |
|      |        |                |               |
|      |        |                |               |
|      |        |                |               |
|      |        |                |               |
|      |        |                |               |
|      |        |                |               |
|      |        |                |               |
|      |        |                |               |
|      |        |                |               |
|      |        |                |               |
|      |        |                |               |
|      |        |                |               |

# SMALL GROUP PRAYER AND PRAISE REPORT

| DATE | PERSON | PRAYER REQUEST | PRAISE REPORT |
|------|--------|----------------|---------------|
|      |        |                |               |
|      |        |                |               |
|      |        |                |               |
|      |        |                |               |
|      |        |                |               |
|      |        |                |               |
|      |        |                |               |
|      |        |                |               |
|      |        |                |               |
|      |        |                |               |
|      |        |                |               |
|      |        |                |               |

## SMALL GROUP CALENDAR

Healthy groups share responsibilities and group ownership. It might take some time for this to develop. Shared ownership ensures that responsibility for the group doesn't fall to one person. Use the calendar to keep track of social events, mission projects, birthdays, or days off. Complete this calendar at your first or second meeting. Planning ahead will increase attendance and shared ownership.

| DATE | LESSON | LOCATION | FACILITATOR | SNACK OR MEAL |
|------|--------|----------|-------------|---------------|
| 5/4 | Session 2 | Chris and Andrea | Jim Brown | Phil and Karen |
| | | | | |
| | | | | |
| | | | | |
| | | | | |
| | | | | |
| | | | | |
| | | | | |
| | | | | |
| | | | | |
| | | | | |
| | | | | |
| | | | | |
| | | | | |
| | | | | |

# ANSWER KEY

### Session One:
### God, the Holy Spirit

In the Old Testament the Holy Spirit came upon people at <u>various</u> times for <u>specific</u> purposes. He never indwelt anyone <u>permanently</u>.

- Do we have to have an <u>experience</u> to be filled and empowered by the Holy Spirit?

**The Holy Spirit <u>regenerates</u> me.**

- Definition: To give <u>rebirth</u>.
- Before I came to Christ, I was <u>spiritually dead</u>.
- Now I am <u>spiritually alive</u> through the new birth.

### Session Two:
### The Role of the Holy Spirit

**The Holy Spirit <u>baptizes</u> me.**

1. The baptism of the Holy Spirit is the placing of the Christian into the <u>body of Christ</u> and into <u>Christ himself</u>.
2. The baptism of the Holy Spirit is a <u>one-time event</u> occurring at the moment of salvation.
3. The baptism of the Holy Spirit is a <u>universal experience</u> for all believers.

**The Holy Spirit <u>indwells</u> me.**

**The Holy Spirit <u>seals</u> me.**

- Sealing implies <u>ownership</u> and <u>protection</u>.

**The Holy Spirit is the <u>deposit of God's promise</u>.**

### Session Three:
### Truths about Creation

1. The <u>natural</u> man
2. The <u>spiritual</u> man
3. The <u>carnal</u> man

1. The verb used for "filled" is plural, implying <u>all</u> are to be filled.
2. The verb used for "filled" is present tense (be filled), implying <u>repeated action</u>.
3. The verb used for "filled" is passive, implying the filling is something done <u>to you</u>.
4. The verb used for "filled" is imperative, implying <u>a command</u>.

1. *Personal experiences that may or may not accompany filling:*

- <u>Emotionalism</u>
- <u>Exceptional</u> ability
- Personal <u>charisma</u>
- <u>Tranquility</u> of mind and spirit
- Speaking in <u>tongues</u>

2. *False teachings concerning what must accompany filling:*

- <u>Freedom</u> from problems
- Total freedom from <u>temptation</u>
- Sinless <u>perfection</u>

3. *Biblical and universal signs of filling:*

- The <u>gifts</u> of the Spirit
- The <u>fruit</u> of the Spirit
- The <u>power</u> of the Spirit

### Session Four:
### Being Filled with the Holy Spirit

1. *<u>Recognize your thirst</u> for filling and desire it.*

2. *<u>Repent of your</u> sins and receive God's cleansing.*

3. *<u>Yield all of yourself</u> to the Holy Spirit's control.*

- Let Jesus <u>be Lord</u> daily.
- <u>Deny yourself</u> daily.

4. *<u>Trust God</u> to fill you as he said he would*

## NOTES

## KEY VERSES

One of the most effective ways to drive deeply into our lives the principles we are learning in this series is to memorize key Scriptures. For many, memorization is a new concept or one that has been difficult in the past. We encourage you to stretch yourself and try to memorize these four key verses. If possible, memorize these as a group and make them part of your group time. You may cut these apart and carry them in your wallet.

*I have hidden your word in my heart that I might not sin against you.*

Psalm 119:11 (NIV)

**Session One**

*Let the Holy Spirit fill and control you.*

Ephesians 5:18b (NLT)

**Session Two**

*For we were all baptized by one Spirit into one body—whether Jews or Greeks, slave or free—and we were all given the one Spirit to drink.*

1 Corinthians 12:13 (NIV)

**Session Three**

*But the spiritual man has insight into everything, and that bothers and baffles the man of the world, who can't understand him at all.*

1 Corinthians 2:15 (LB)

**Session Four**

*. . . the mind controlled by the Spirit is life and peace.*

Romans 8:6 (NIV)

## NOTES

We value your thoughts about what you've just read.
Please share them with us. You'll find contact information
in the back of this book.

# *The Purpose Driven® Life*
# A six-session video-based study for groups or individuals

Embark on a journey of discovery with this video-based study taught by Rick Warren. In it you will discover the answer to life's most fundamental question: "What on earth am I here for?"

And here's a clue to the answer: It's not about you . . . You were created by God and for God, and until you understand that, life will never make sense. It is only in God that we discover our origin, our identity, our meaning, our purpose, our significance, and our destiny."

Whether you experience this adventure with a small group or on your own, this six-session, video-based study will change your life.

DVD Study Guide: 978-0-310-27866-5
DVD: 978-0-310-27864-1

Be sure to combine this study with your reading of the best-selling book, *The Purpose Driven® Life*, to give you or your small group the opportunity to discuss the implications and applications of living the life God created you to live.

Hardcover, Jacketed: 978-0-310-20571-5
Softcover: 978-0-310-27699-9

Pick up a copy today at your favorite bookstore!

**ZONDERVAN®**
.com

# Foundations: 11 Core Truths to Build Your Life On

## Taught by Tom Holladay and Kay Warren

*Foundations* is a series of 11 four-week video studies covering the most important, foundational doctrines of the Christian faith. Study topics include:

**The Bible**—This study focuses on where the Bible came from, why it can be trusted, and how it can change your life.

DVD Study Guide: 978-0-310-27670-8
DVD: 978-0-310-27669-2

**God**—This study focuses not just on facts about God, but on how to know God himself in a more powerful and personal way.

DVD Study Guide: 978-0-310-27672-2
DVD: 978-0-310-27671-5

**Jesus**—As we look at what the Bible says about the person of Christ, we do so as people who are developing a lifelong relationship with Jesus.

DVD Study Guide: 978-0-310-27676-0
DVD: 978-0-310-27675-3

**The Holy Spirit**—This study focuses on the person, the presence, and the power of the Holy Spirit, and how you can be filled with the Holy Spirit on a daily basis.

DVD Study Guide: 978-0-310-27676-0
DVD: 978-0-310-27675-3

**Creation**—Each of us was personally created by a loving God. This study does not shy away from the great scientific and theological arguments that surround the creation/ evolution debate. However, you will find the goal of this study is deepening your awareness of God as your Creator.

DVD Study Guide: 978-0-310-27678-4
DVD: 978-0-310-27677-7

Pick up a copy today at your favorite bookstore!

ZONDERVAN®
.com

**Salvation**—This study focuses on God's solution to man's need for salvation, what Jesus Christ did for us on the cross, and the assurance and security of God's love and provision for eternity.

DVD Study Guide: 978-0-310-27682-1
DVD: 978-0-310-27679-1

**Sanctification**—This study focuses on the two natures of the Christian. We'll see the difference between grace and law, and how these two things work in our lives.

DVD Study Guide: 978-0-310-27684-5
DVD: 978-0-310-27683-8

**Good and Evil**—Why do bad things happen to good people? Through this study we'll see how and why God continues to allow evil to exist. The ultimate goal is to build up our faith and relationship with God as we wrestle with these difficult questions.

DVD Study Guide: 978-0-310-27687-6
DVD: 978-0-310-27686-9

**The Afterlife**—The Bible does not answer all the questions we have about what happens to us after we die; however, this study deals with what the Bible does tell us. This important study gives us hope and helps us move from a focus on the here and now to a focus on eternity.

DVD Study Guide: 978-0-310-27689-0
DVD: 978-0-310-27688-3

**The Church**—This study focuses on the birth of the church, the nature of the church, and the mission of the church.

DVD Study Guide: 978-0-310-27692-0
DVD: 978-0-310-27691-3

**The Second Coming**—This study addresses both the hope and the uncertainties surrounding the second coming of Jesus Christ.

DVD Study Guide: 978-0-310-27695-1
DVD: 978-0-310-27693-7

Pick up a copy today at your favorite bookstore!

**ZONDERVAN**®
.com

# Celebrate Recovery, Updated Curriculum Kit

This kit will provide your church with the tools necessary to start a successful Celebrate Recovery program. *Kit includes:*

- Introductory Guide for Leaders DVD
- Leader's Guide
- 4 Participant's Guides (one of each guide)
- CD-ROM with 25 lessons
- CD-ROM with sermon transcripts
- 4-volume audio CD sermon series

Curriculum Kit: 978-0-310-26847-5

## Participant's Guide 4-pack

The Celebrate Recovery Participant's Guide 4-pack is a convenient resource when you're just getting started or if you need replacement guides for your program.

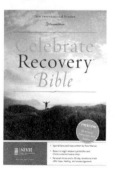

## Celebrate Recovery Bible

With features based on eight principles Jesus voiced in his Sermon on the Mount, the new *Celebrate Recovery Bible* offers hope, encouragement, and empowerment for those struggling with the circumstances of their lives and the habits they are trying to control.

Hardcover 978-0-310-92849-2
Softcover 978-0-310-93810-1

Pick up a copy today at your favorite bookstore!

### Stepping Out of Denial into God's Grace

Participant's Guide 1 introduces the eight principles of recovery based on Jesus' words in the Beatitudes, and focuses on principles 1–3. Participants learn about denial, hope, sanity, and more.

### Getting Right with God, Yourself, and Others

Participant's Guide 3 covers principles 5–7 based on Jesus' words in the Beatitudes. With courage and support from their fellow participants, people seeking recovery will find victory, forgiveness, and grace.

### Taking an Honest and Spiritual Inventory

Participant's Guide 2 focuses on the fourth principle based on Jesus' words in the Beatitudes and builds on the Scripture, *"Happy are the pure in heart."* (Matthew 5:8) The participant will learn an invaluable principle for recovery and also take an in-depth spiritual inventory.

### Growing in Christ While Helping Others

Participant's Guide 4 walks through the final steps of the eight recovery principles based on Jesus' words in the Beatitudes. In this final phase, participants learn to move forward in newfound freedom in Christ, learning how to give back to others. There's even a practical lesson called "Seven reasons we get stuck in our recoveries."

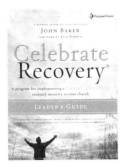

## Leader's Guide

The Celebrate Recovery Leader's Guide gives you everything you need to facilitate your preparation time. Virtually walking you through every meeting, the Leader's Guide is a must-have for every leader on your Celebrate Recovery ministry team.

Pick up a copy today at your favorite bookstore!

# Wide Angle:
# Framing Your Worldview

Christianity is much more than a religion. It is a worldview—a way of seeing all of life and the world around you. Your worldview impacts virtually every decision you make in life: moral decisions, relational decisions, financial decisions— everything. How you see the world determines how you face the world.

In this brand new study, Rick Warren and Chuck Colson discuss such key issues as moral relativism, tolerance, terrorism, creationism vs. Darwinism, sin and suffering. They explore in depth the Christian worldview as it relates to the most important questions in life:

- Why does it matter what I believe?
- How do I know what's true?
- Where do I come from?
- Why is the world so messed up?
- Is there a solution?
- What is my purpose in life?

This study is as deep as it is wide, addressing vitally important topics for every follower of Christ.

*Rick Warren*

*Chuck Colson*

DVD Study Guide: 978-1-4228-0083-6
DVD: 978-1-4228-0082-9

# The Way of a Worshiper

The pursuit of God is the chase of a lifetime—in fact, it's been going on since the day you were born. The question is: Have you been the hunter or the prey?

This small group study is not about music. It's not even about going to church. It's about living your life as an offering of worship to God. It's about tapping into the source of power to live the Christian life. And it's about discovering the secret to friendship with God.

In these four video sessions, Buddy Owens helps you unpack the meaning of worship. Through his very practical, engaging, and at times surprising insights, Buddy shares truths from Scripture and from life that will help you understand in a new and deeper way just what it means to be a worshiper.

God is looking for worshipers. His invitation to friendship is open and genuine. Will you take him up on his offer? Will you give yourself to him in worship? Then come walk *The Way of a Worshiper* and discover the secret to friendship with God.

DVD Study Guide: 978-1-4228-0096-6
DVD: 978-1-4228-0095-9

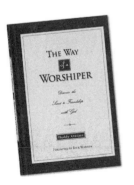

## THE WAY of a WORSHIPER

Your study of this material will be greatly enhanced by reading the book, *The Way of a Worshiper: Discover the Secret to Friendship with God.*

# Managing Our Finances God's Way

Did you know that there are over 2,350 verses in the Bible about money? Did you know that nearly half of Jesus' parables are about possessions? The Bible is packed with wise counsel about your financial life. In fact, Jesus had more to say about money than about heaven and hell combined.

Introducing a new video-based small group study that will inspire you to live debt free! Created by Saddleback Church and Crown Financial Ministries, learn what the Bible has to say about our finances from Rick Warren, Chip Ingram, Ron Blue, Howard Dayton, and Chuck Bentley as they address important topics like:

- God's Solution to Debt
- Saving and Investing
- Plan Your Spending
- Giving as an Act of Worship
- Enjoy What God has Given You

*Study includes:*

- DVD with seven 20-minute lessons

- Workbook with seven lessons

- Resource CD with digital version of all worksheets that perform calculations automatically

- Contact information for help with answering questions

- Resources for keeping financial plans on track and making them lifelong habits

NOTE: PARTICIPANTS DO NOT SHARE PERSONAL FINANCIAL INFORMATION WITH EACH OTHER.

DVD Study Guide: 978-1-4228-0083-6
DVD: 978-1-4228-0082-9

ines the old lady's hands plopping one bead on the other in the days when Gorkey's General was new and her long braid was blonde.

The old lady's hair went silver the day Fran arrived. She put herself to bed to die the day Cora was born.

Despite the comforts of the internal stairs, Fran refuses to use them. "We live above Gorkey, not with him. Using the inside stairs might confuse the way people view my connection to him." Fran has explained this to Cora many times. Cora understands how Fran's past is tainted, knows how committed Fran is to preserving the respect the townsfolk have for Gorkey and the old lady. "Got to keep us separate so there's no temptation to paint them with the same damned brush. Gorkey took us in, Cora, and that's enough. No sense in doing anything to get folks talking."

And if Cora told her how grey, how dull and boring the people of Little Cypress thought their lives were, would Fran be relieved? Would she use the internal stairs?

Among the Chore Boys and dishwashing liquid at the back of the store, women tell Cora just how much they see of how she and her mother live. Contemplating the price of Spic and Span, the women discuss Cora and Fran's lives, while Cora, behind the thin wall, pretends to have fallen asleep reading to old Mrs. Gorkey.

The old lady likes advertisements and product descriptions best, likes Cora to read them aloud from catalogues mailed to Gorkey's General. Old Mrs. Gorkey closes her eyes, folds her hands over her chest in death position and listens to Cora. Cora strokes the old lady's shoulder, ignores her curiously sweet scent and reads to her fifty-nine-year-old body. "For the first time science has found a new healing substance with the astonishing ability to shrink hemorrhoids and to relieve pain—without surgery. Most amazing of all—results were so thorough that sufferers made astonishing statements like 'Piles have ceased to be a problem!'" Cora watches the smile sneak across the old lady's face, thumbs through the catalogue, pauses. "Here's a thing. A new sanitary belt! 'Now Kotex has Wondersoft covering. This new open-mesh covering is incredibly light and gentle. To complete your comfort, Kotex has created a new sanitary belt. Soft, flexible clasps put an end to cutting and chafing.'"

But when two or more of the town's women congregate near the back of the store, looking for Comet, Cora often lets her eyes flicker, lets her head dip against her chest until sleep seems to overtake her. She curls up on the old lady's bed, locks her arms over Mrs. Gorkey's aged thighs, soft as uncooked sausages, and listens to the women on the other side of the wall. The old lady braids Cora's hair and resists coughing.

The women talk about Jane's color scheme, how her wallpaper with orange flowers on a brown background and her sofa blend *just perfectly*. They discuss the price and capacity of Laura's *brand-spanking-new* deep freeze; they talk about how Samantha's skirt lifted in that *swell* way when she danced with Ted at the last cocktail party and how *smashed Tony was. Did you see him roll out the door? I thought he'd pull poor Tammy down with him when he stumbled like that.*

Cora prefers the occasions when she and Fran are the topic of discussion, especially when Winnie's at it. Winnie McRae, the barber's wife. Nothing Winnie likes better than to speculate on Fran and Cora McLellan. The two of them, together with *Woman's Home Companion* and lipstick, are her particular weakness.

"What a wonderful day," Cora hears her say to Stella Johnson, the doctor's wife. The two of them are at the back of the store pretending to compare furniture polish prices. "The sky's just bluer than blue."

"Yes. Nice. Johnstone's is cheaper."

"No, it's four cents more than Pledge."

"If you check the volume, Winnie, you'll see there's less polish. But you're right about the day. We're going on a picnic. . . ."

"Who? Who's going?"

"Now, just give me a minute. We'd never leave you out, Winnie. I was about to invite you."

"Well, I'll have to think about it. Who's going?"

"Mari and little Elwood, Flury, and if you want, you and your girls."

"He wouldn't want to come, would he?"

"Who? Flury?"

"Isn't he too old for picnics? How old is he now, seventeen?"

"It's his father's idea. Flury tells me he feels silly being dragged around with me, but his father insists. He can spend his time flying kites or with me. And you can't fly kites every day of the summer, you know."

"No, I guess that gets boring. Being alone like that up the hill."

"Well, it keeps him away from the storefront. His father won't have him hanging out here in front of Gorkey's with the other kids."

"I've changed my mind."

"What?"

"Flury's not too old for picnics. Thank goodness his father's keeping an eye on him. It's dreadful the way those boys wiggle their hips, all of them with that thick-lipped pout. Have you heard those boys singing?"

"Yes, Winnie. But they're not bad kids, really."

"If they're not, they will be. *Love me tender.* What's that suppose to mean? You just watch them roll their eyes. Songs like that are giving them ideas. I walk past them and can just tell by their eyes that they'd like to eat the pearls from my neck. Your husband's absolutely right. I'm surprised he hasn't written an article about it."

"He will. I'm sure of it. You watch. He'll be suggesting that all young men fly kites, like 'Joe Teenager.' I don't know why Edgar insists on calling Flury that in his articles. Everyone knows Joe Teenager is really his son. Are you coming?"

"Where?"

"On the picnic."

"Of course."

"How does the pond sound?"

"What?"

"The picnic, Winnie. We can paddle around in Charlemaigne's boat. Imagine owning that boat for all these years and never going near it."

"Mmmmm. Must be easier than taking the trouble of selling. Anyway, the pond sounds heavenly. Days like this, when we're off picnicking, I think of Fran. Look at the poor thing—in here weighing vegetables in that dull little corner. I tell you, if I had to work, I'd work in a women's clothing store, thank-you very much. Heavens, anything would be better than this."

"Leave it," says Stella. "You're always wanting to talk about Fran."

"Well, Stella, I have a heart. I care. Look at that child. She's a young woman. Must be over sixteen and her mother hasn't bought her so much as a tube of lipstick let alone a bra."

"Winnie, that's none of our business."

"If Cora were my daughter, I'd buy her one of those nifty single-strap bathing suits I saw in the *Woman's Home Companion* or a little shirt with a Peter Pan collar. But, oh no, Fran doesn't buy her a thing. Poor thing, lost in these dark aisles, shy as all get-out."

"Maybe she doesn't want a bra or a swimsuit, Winnie."

"Stella, all girls her age want those things. But she's so mousy, she likely hasn't told her mother what she wants. Surely Fran could guess that she wants lipstick. It might liven her up a bit, make her want to talk. Sad quiet thing, bent over tin cans, writing prices, and I really can't think who her father could be. Not that we'd know him, of course, but I've always wondered what he looks like. Really. Do you think he knows that he has a daughter who works in a general store? I mean, look at her. Lord knows she doesn't take after her mother, who's getting so—"

"Winnie, talk about something else."

"Fine. But just let me say, and I'd only say it to you, Stella, I wouldn't wish Fran's life on anyone."

"You always say that. You just hate to say it, but you always do."

"You wouldn't catch me working my life away in this dull place. If I had to work I'd be an airline stewardess with those little A-lines and a matching hat. Or I'd even work at the A&W."

"Winnie—"

"Yes, Stella?"

"If you had a baby and no father to help raise that baby, there's no way you'd be a stewardess."

"The point is I wouldn't have kept the baby."

"Just leave it, Winnie."

"She should have put Cora up for adoption. With adoption, everyone wins. No one had to know about Fran's baby. If she'd just gone home and left the baby here, everything would have been fine. She could have waited a year or two, got married. Then she'd be having coffee Tuesday mornings instead of working all day and into the night in this place. And Cora would likely have a bra. And lipstick."

"Leave it alone, Winnie. Think of what Cora means to her."

"Fran's paying. Every single minute, she's paying for her decision."

"It can't be so bad, really."

"No? Tin cans to stack and an oilwood floor to sweep and the old lady in the back who won't quit coughing and a three-legged stool to prop her behind against when it's quiet in the evenings and a dull room upstairs. Should I whip up a potato salad for our picnic?"

It's about here in the conversation that Cora starts wriggling against the old lady's legs. She rubs her eyes, checks for the smile on the old lady's face. Finished braiding Cora's hair, the old lady ties a green satin ribbon around it, then drops the heavy skein against the bedspread.

Lying on her back, Cora looks up to the flickering of wild birds Gorkey has fashioned from the pages of his mother's magazines. Gorkey ties strings to the birds, pins them to the ceiling. They whirl, vivid as paradise. Gorkey's thin hands can make anything.

Midmorning, Gorkey flips the sign in the front window of the store to CLOSED (but doesn't lock up, customers still come in, still shop, wait the fifteen minutes to pay) and slips through the beaded curtain with Fran. At the end of the hall a door opens to a courtyard unseen from the alley. In this fragrant space, alive with sunlight and the watermelon-colored begonias Fran grows, they sit and drink their morning coffee. On summer break, Cora joins them. Gorkey hums Polish tunes the old lady taught him, while the water on the stove comes to a boil. Gorkey pours the hot liquid into a mug and adds a Red Rose tea bag for Fran, then brings a small container of fresh cream from the cooler to pour into their tea. Fran leans back against the linden tree and thumbs through the old lady's magazines. She pauses and, having chosen, tears out a page and hands it to Gorkey.

"Close your eyes," he says. In the silence his hands come to life. He unfurls the fingers of his left hand, releasing his cocooned thumb with its long and curled nail. His thin fingers flicker, bend and fold, move the paper first this way, then that. With his thumbnail he slices deftly. "Okay, Fran," he says, his voice soft as the cotton balls on the pharmacy shelf. She puts out her hand, and he releases a wild bird, color winging against her palm.

Cora opens her eyes, pulls herself from the old lady's bed with Winnie and Stella's words fresh in her mind. She sits on a chair beside the old lady's bed. Picks up the half-read magazine. "Electric blankets to match any decor," she reads aloud.

"If his father had him flying kites, you would have met him," old lady Gorkey says.

"Who?"

The old lady closes her eyes. Won't tolerate games. The old lady knows that there is only one place to fly kites, only one place where the wind rushes freely. Up Little Cypress Hill.

From the hill, Cora sees women hanging laundry in their backyards, watches the cool cats who hang around Gorkey's storefront in the summertime heat. The girls whirl Hula-Hoops—red, yellow and blue—round their hips, lift their hands to their hair, the hoops still circling, until the boys break into a love-me-tender tune.

Words glide up the hill . . . *love me sweet* . . . up up, Cora's eyes catching sight of the kite which flies high . . . *and never let me go.* Voices from the boys below urging her to follow the kite string, down down through the sky to the boy who holds it.

*Flury*

KUMQUAT, the color of tangerine on his lips. Orange-gold and round as a pearl. Eggplant. Mango. Flury rolls over in his bed, hears the wind whirling through the apple tree outside his window. "Kumquat," he whispers.

The wind outside Flury's window ceases briefly, and in that moment, he hears the squeak of his father's chair. Saturday morning, thinks Flury. He'll be writing an article for his weekly column, "What the Doctor Says," by Edward P. Johnson, MD. What, wonders Flury, will the doctor say today? Perhaps more about Mrs. Winnie McRae, the barber's wife, who so impresses his father because she is on so many committees.

Flury's father maintains that articles which applaud positive behavior have a positive effect on the community. "My articles give people hints on proper behavior. Here in Little Cypress, people tend to want my approval, so they generally emulate the behavior I recognize as correct. That'll be you, one day, son."

"Example Set by Outstanding Community Lady" headlined last week's article. "A strong volunteer base provides the foundation for a healthy and vibrant community. Volunteers ensure that such worthwhile societies as the Red Cross and the PTA run smoothly. Mrs. Frank McRae is a shining example of a very active volunteer in our community. 'I like to volunteer,' says Mrs. McRae. She wisely notes, however, that 'Homemaking comes first with me.' Proverbs 17:1 says, 'Better is a dry morsel, and quietness therewith, than an house full of sacrifices with strife.' Mrs. McRae added that she believes all brides-to-be should pass a cooking test before they can obtain their marriage license."

Flury closes his eyes, imagines the smell of the leather chair in the early morning, hears it creak under his weight. He sees himself lift his pen, tap it on his teeth. *Kumquat. Papaya.* Flury pulls the blankets over his face. In the darkness he imagines the men outside Frank's Barbershop waiting for a shave or haircut. *That Dr. Flury, he's right, you know.* Flury wiggles his toes. *Vermicelli.*

~

"Vermicelli," Cora says to him up Little Cypress Hill, "looks like transparent thread, the material that ties angels to our shoulders. They float up there in the darkness with these thin see-through threads that run from them to our right shoulders. There," she says, touching his shoulder, "that's where you're attached."

"She'll order anything," Cora continues. "The old lady gets catalogues from all over the world, and anything that's offered, she'll order. Really. I'll be reading to her. 'Stop,' she'll say. 'Read it again.' So I do. 'Ti Plant Log from Hawaii! No green thumb needed! Just place Hawaiian Ti Plant Log in water and watch it grow. A luxuriant, rare Polynesian plant with 1001 uses!' 'Perfect,' she tells me. 'Fran can grow it in the courtyard.' So we send off our dollar for two logs, and before you know it, Fran's got Ti logs growing alongside her begonias."

Cora stretches the green ribbon between her hands, lowers

her mouth, begins to nibble it in half, then stops. "She likes stuff she can eat. Gets a kick out of Fran selling potatoes out front while she eats star anise in the back. In the days when the old lady still worked the till, she tried to get people to eat avocados or rutabaga, but no way."

~

It's not working. Flury's not getting excited about the articles he intends to write when he grows up. Today, with the wind outside his window making his thoughts fly off like a thousand birds, there are no words.

But then, are there words after *vermicelli*, after *angel tethers?* How can "It is wise to conclude that children are the pioneers of adventure as long as the adventure is accompanied by an adult" compare with the power of *Aubergine?* The sound of *avocado?*

~

"She turned green once."

"What?"

"Yeah, the old lady did."

He wants to laugh. Lowers his head to the kite he holds.

"Really." Cora puts out her hand, lifts his head. "You can laugh. It's okay. It's funny. She laughed too. She's always laughing."

"How. How'd she turn green?"

"Avocados. She took a huge liking to them. It happens, you know. If you eat too many carrots you turn orange. And she turned green from avocados. Her skin's white as roots under a fallen log from never being outside, so the green was really obvious."

He watches her nibble at her ribbon. "So how many avocados do you have to eat before you turn green?"

"Tons. For days. She's like that. The price was right so she ordered six dozen. Thing is, they get overripe fast. So she had to eat them all up before they rotted. Which wasn't a problem because she really likes them. For two weeks we were planting avocado seeds and tossing out avocado skins while she sat in her bed with a spoon. And then she turned green."

Flury gives himself to the humor and cracks a smile. "That's good," he says. But then, watching her chew on her green ribbon, seeing her small teeth scissor the satin, he can't resist asking, "Is it true?"

She stops chewing. Looks up at him. "Oh yes, entirely true."

"I just wondered."

"It's okay. Fran's always worried I'll start to confuse what I've made up with what happens. But I'm quite clear about it."

"That's good."

"Like the shopping sprees to California, for instance. Those are made up. We never went. But the avocados are true."

"That's what I thought."

"She has the dresses though. The old lady really has tropical dresses, and she looks great in them. But we never actually leave Gorkey's. She's got three of those dresses with wild birds and strange plants. I found them in a catalogue, and she liked the colors so much she ordered three. 'Slip on your beach dress,' I tell her. So we put on our sunglasses, and I wiggle into the nifty single-strap bathing suit she ordered for me, and we're on our way to the freshest avocados the old lady's ever tasted and an ocean blue as any bluebell. But we don't go anywhere."

"I didn't think so," he says. He takes a bit of ribbon from her and sits down to tie it to the tail of his kite. The ribbon is damp on his hands. Flury takes a breath and speaks, his voice quieter than he intends. "I've never seen her. Never seen the old lady."

Cora shrugs and starts chewing another bit of ribbon. "A lot of people haven't."

"I mean, is that her doing all that coughing?"

Cora pulls at the ribbon where her teeth have frayed the fabric. "Yes, that's her."

"My father says she's waiting to die."

"Maybe she is."

"My father says she's crazy for dropping out of life like that. She should have been a mother to Gorkey instead of lying in a dark room waiting for him to bring her chicken soup. A son needs a mother and a father. And by deciding to die, she left Gorkey with no one. Which, says my father, is very irresponsible."

"You don't have a clue what you're talking about."

"Well, it sounds weird to me."

"She just wants Gorkey to be happy. Which, in her opinion, means she's got to die." Cora drops a torn piece of ribbon on his lap, pulls her hair back and ties what is left of the ribbon around her hair. "What else does your daddy say? Bet he's managed to tell you that Fran's a loose woman, hasn't he? Bet he's whispered 'Like mother, like daughter' to you when you've passed by Gorkey's and seen me at the till."

"Not exactly. But he's quoted Ecclesiastes, which says, 'The thing that hath been, it is that which shall be; and that which is done is that which shall be done: and there is no new thing under the sun.'"

"Which means?"

"Like mother, like daughter, I suppose."

Cora bends down, picks an overripe raspberry. She looks at it for a moment, then squashes it with surprising strength in the middle of his forehead.

"What?" he says, pulling her hand from his face. "Cut it out!" He wipes his forehead with the back of his hand. Stares at the red juice, drags his hand through the grass to remove the stain.

"What a waste of a perfectly good raspberry," says Cora. She drops to her knees. Takes one lick of his forehead, then turns and, laughing into the sky, begins to run, her long blonde hair swishing across her back.

"What's so funny?" he calls out.

"I got the last lick." And she holds her tummy, doubles over, before disappearing behind a gravestone.

Flury, still feeling the quick rasp of Cora's tongue on his forehead, thinks, Strange, she's totally and entirely strange.

~

Flury, hearing the swirl of wind in the apple tree's branches, recalls the way Cora animal-licked him and then vanished into the graveyard. Something is making him agitated. He's hot. Cold. There is nowhere to stretch his limbs. It's the damned wind, he thinks, constantly rubbing against his thoughts like a cat against his leg.

Why should it bother him that Cora knew about his father's whispers? Why, just because Cora divulged the old lady's eccentricities, should it make him wish he could deny his father quoting Ecclesiastes? There is comfort, Flury reminds himself, in being the son of a man who understands the past, who can anticipate patterns. Like father, like son. Why, on this windy morning, would he long for the chance to apologize to the girl who licked his forehead?

The wind. Damn wind. Flury rises from his bed, moves to his open window. But before closing it he recalls the feel of Cora's tongue on his skin. He lifts his kite from the shelf, listening to be certain his father is still in his study. Then carefully he removes the cloth he has wrapped around the kite's tail and touches the ribbon from Cora's hair.

A good day for kite flying.

*Cora*

CORA LISTENS TO THE AWNING above Gorkey's storefront snap over and over in the wind. The old lady coughs and Cora lifts her head from beneath the quilt she shares with Fran. She twists her head around until she sees Fran's reflection in the bathroom mirror. "You don't have to take the fire escape," she says to Fran. "Why bother? Too windy if you ask me."

"We live above," says Fran, "not with." Cora mimics Fran's words, watches Fran bend to her nylons, which hang over the edge of the tub like thin and exhausted dancers.

"What's the diff?"

"Between what and what?"

"Above and with."

Fran, seeing Cora's reflection in the mirror, lifts an eyebrow. Opens her mouth with an exasperated I've-told-you-a-million-times look.

"Just forget it." Cora knows full well that despite the wind Fran will take the fire escape, just like every other morning, at seven in full view of Frank's Barbershop.

As if Frank comes to work that early in the morning just so he can watch Fran walk down the fire escape. As if, later, when Winnie pops in to drop off her groceries, he'll say, "Well, Winnie, my love, Fran took the fire escape again. Didn't take the internal stairs."

Winnie, straightening his tie will nod, "And a good thing that is too." Then she'll point to his shirt tails, her auburn eyebrow lifting.

With a melting smile, Frank will bend to Winnie and try to kiss her stern brow before she turns away.

Cora tries to imagine the conversation that would follow, but what do Frank and Winnie talk about? They've got nothing in common, thinks Cora. Frank, with his pink cheeks and soft belly, can spend an afternoon humming one tune after another on the bench in front of his shop, while Winnie, with her committee commitments, attacks her day like a wasp at a picnic. Despite Winnie's obvious attempts to keep Frank in newly pressed trousers and a starched white shirt daily, Frank looks as though he's got monkey bars in the back of his shop and sets to playing on them as soon as Winnie's out of sight.

Fran, Cora knows, will step into the wind and take the fire escape. Around the corner, behind the red and peeling front door of Gorkey's General, Gorkey will hear her brief knock. And, as Cora has witnessed for as long as she's lived, Gorkey will open the door, his long fingers reaching for Fran's hand. "Good morning, Fran," he'll say, a note of surprise in his voice, as though she hadn't worked for him for seventeen years.

"Something in that wind all right," Fran says, stepping out of the bathroom with her white gloves under her arm, nylons in her hands. She watches Cora lift her hair from her neck, tie it with a frayed bit of green ribbon. Fran begins to put on her gloves, lifts her nose to the air like a dog. Sniffs, then asks again, "What're you up to today?"

"You already asked."

"You never answered."

"That's because," says Cora, "my options haven't changed. I read to the old lady or go up the hill. Thing is though, Miss Charlemaigne with her dumb dead-butterfly collection has left her bench by the bakery and has begun hanging around the graveyard."

Fran isn't listening. She sniffs again.

"Would you forget the damned wind!"

"Can't you smell it, Cora? Even from there?"

Cora watches her mother return to the bathroom, rises from their bed and moves quickly to the window. Drops her head to the three holes at the windowsill.

Flury's feet. Cora sees Flury's white feet in a tangle of wild raspberries, bare and so clean they seem new as day. Laced with veins as delicate as embroidery. The apple-sauce scent of the wind gives her unaccustomed clarity. Cora knows his naked feet are an initial act of defiance.

"I'll probably be a doctor," he says, spooling his kite string to the expanse of sky. "Like father, like son." He glances back at her.

Cora plucks wild grass from its thick sheath, eats the white end. "You must feel silly going on picnics with your mother."

"What?"

"Yeah. You must."

"What did you say?"

"You're too old for picnics."

He taps his foot. "My father tells me these are the hardest years. If I can steer clear of trouble now, my father says, I'll end up ahead." He looks at her. "Y'know. Ahead of the others."

"The kids outside Gorkey's?"

"Yeah. Them. As my father says, 'He that diggeth a pit shall fall into it.' Ecclesiastes 10:8."

"Oh," says Cora.

"Well, it's true. People our age need to keep their minds sharp and their bodies healthy. Outdoor activities—"

"Like picnics—"

"Well, that's better than spending time in the dingy back rooms of Gorkey's."

"You mean," she says, "where the old lady won't quit coughing and a mother with no morals has enough fat on her behind to sink a ship? Where Gorkey shuffles around in the dim light like a zombie? That's what you'll have heard." She shakes her head, tries not to smile.

He looks toward her in the bright light. "What's so funny?"

Cora shrugs. "Just fly your kite," she says.

"Really, I want to know. What's so funny?"

She bites her lower lip, wishes he would quit looking at her so intensely. Cora turns. "Your kite's dipping."

He walks backward, away from her, his feet shuffling through the raspberries. He lifts a bare foot to the shin of his other leg, wipes the sole of his foot against his trousers. Then he looks down, watching red bleed across the white fabric. He looks up at her, making certain she has seen. Then he smiles.

Cora pulls from the window, snaps the wooden bar over the three holes and thinks of a kite with green satin ribbon tied to its tail in bows.

Cora knows by the way Fran angles her body slowly around

to ask again, "Where did you say you were going?" that she is moved by the fragrant wind.

"Can't you just drop it?"

"Why?"

"Why, all of a sudden, is it so important what I'm up to? I'll either read to the old lady or sit in the graveyard up Little Cypress with Miss Charlemaigne touching my neck when I'm not looking or wanting to tie bows in my hair. Okay? One or the other. Why's it suddenly such a big deal?"

Fran leans against the bathroom doorframe. She takes a deep breath and holds it. Lifts her eyes to the window and, letting her breath melt slowly from her body, says, "Could be a fine day for flying a kite."

Cora stares at Fran.

"It's nice up there, isn't it, when the wind's big? And you feel like you can see forever."

Cora returns to the bed. Pulls her knees to her chest, pokes her head back into the warm cocoon beneath her nightie. She looks at the shadow triangle between her legs and whispers inside her head, The old lady has told Fran. Clearly. Either her or Miss Charlemaigne. Someone has told Fran how he might look, arms high to the sky as though in flight, his feet bare, his white soles stained red with the juice of raspberries.

There is no doubt that Miss Charlemaigne knows too. Fuddy-dud school teacher. Thick-ankled butterfly collector. The woman who wanders about with a net over her shoulder and too many words in her mouth.

Miss Charlemaigne insists on sitting on the stone beside Cora. Tells Cora facts about her beloved Lepidoptera as she drops the butterflies she has collected into a jar containing an ether-soaked ball of cotton. Miss Charlemaigne watches them die as she speaks.

She knows, thinks Cora, dipping her head deeper into her nightie. No doubt about it.

~

"Mimicry," says Miss Charlemaigne. "Let me tell you about mimicry. There's a lesson here somewhere. Now I just happen to have caught what I believe to be a painted lady. Rare. Very rare to see one in these parts. I'll have to compare her to the photo in my book once I have her pinned. Anyway, take a look at this butterfly. Here."

Cora doesn't want to take the jar Miss Charlemaigne hands her and is repelled by the slow flutter of the orange butterfly. But once she looks, Cora can't resist the beauty of black wing veins singed onto orange powder, a pattern like lead in a stained glass window. Along the margins of the wing, white dots, pure as snow.

When Cora returns the jar, Miss Charlemaigne brushes her hand against Cora's and shifts her body in Cora's direction. Cora shifts away.

Miss Charlemaigne moves her eyes to Cora's face, opens her mouth to speak, but doesn't.

"Go on," says Cora. "Mimicry. The painted lady."

"Yes, mimicry. So this painted lady, see, she doesn't feed on milkweed like the monarch. And the monarch is noxious to birds because of milkweed." She stops talking and looks into the distance.

Cora follows Miss Charlemaigne's gaze. Sees the very top of his head appear in the distance. "Go on, Miss Charlemaigne, so what about the milkweed?"

"It's poison to birds. A bird eats a monarch who eats milkweed and it dies. Mmmmm. Either dies or gets sick. Milkweed is noxious, and that's why the monarch's so bright."

Cora watches as he strides up the hill, his hair the color of tree bark. First his face and then his shoulders, his arms extended carefully, carrying his kite like a child with a new toy.

"I know him," says Miss Charlemaigne. "He's the doctor's son."

They watch as he stops a distance away, bends down to untie his shoelaces.

Miss Charlemaigne pulls her eyes from him, says, "You don't know him?"

Cora says, "Now this butterfly, the one in the jar. You think it's a painted lady?"

"Can't say for sure. Not yet. But if it is, then it's evolved to look like a monarch, you see. It's bright orange because the monarch is. A bird could spot a monarch anywhere. Their brightness says catch something else for dinner. Smart, huh?"

"Yeah." Cora nods without looking at Miss Charlemaigne. Now barefoot, he stands on the edge of the hill, holding his kite up to the wind. She squints, wants to see him better, wants to watch as his fingers open, letting his new kite learn the wind.

"So the painted lady, looking like the monarch, scares birds away, although she's not at all noxious."

He lifts a wet finger to the wind. Waiting, Cora knows, for the seventh gust.

~

"It's stupid," he says, "but why shouldn't the wind be like waves? If the seventh wave is always the biggest, then it makes sense the seventh gust should be bigger too. So I wait for the seventh gust."

"Is that true? About waves?"

"Sure. So if the seventh wave is the biggest then that bigness must come from somewhere, maybe from wind gusts. The seventh."

"What was that one?"

"Four. Just wait, you'll see. My father says patience is a virtue."

"Was it his idea to keep your string like that?"

"Looks good, huh? Makes it nice and even on the spool. Nothing worse than tangled string. Okay, that's five."

"Did your father tell you about the wind gusts too?"

He lowers his kite and puts it under his arm. "What are you getting at?"

"Well, most the stuff you say comes from your father."

"The wind gust thing—it's mine, okay? That's my idea. All my own."

"It's good. A good idea."

He looks at her.

"Come on. Let's see how it does in the seventh gust," says Cora.

"I have thoughts of my own. Interests, you know, that aren't his."

"Okay. I just wondered, that's all."

"I mean, I may be his son, but . . ."

Cora looks up at him and nods. Then she bends down to pluck a just-ripe raspberry and puts it in her mouth.

"You should wash that. Really. Who knows what's on it."

Cora tries not to laugh. Doesn't want the red of the raspberry running from the corners of her mouth. Doesn't want to see his hurt.

"It's not funny."

"Okay, it's not. Now let's see that seventh gust get this kite into the sky."

~

Miss Charlemaigne touches Cora's thigh. "You're not listening."

"Yes, I am."

"So the painted lady dresses herself up like the monarch. Birds stay clear of her too."

"Good," says Cora, watching his kite lift.

Then so does he. Yes. Open-armed he is pulled skyward. He drifts above the green hedges and the laundry hanging on the lines. He flies above the women who visit on front porches and over hedges. He soars past the boys and girls who sing Elvis out loud.

Miss Charlemaigne rises from the stone. She moves toward him, pulled by an invisible thread. She steps carefully, holding her breath.

Cora follows.

"I just want a better look at him," Miss Charlemaigne whispers. "Look how he appears to be flying. Now, isn't that interesting." Miss Charlemaigne pauses.

"What?"

Miss Charlemaigne turns to Cora and rolls her eyes. "He's got ribbon that matches yours on the tail of his kite."

Cora shrugs.

"Y'know," says Miss Charlemaigne, her body stilled, watching, "he looks like his father, his face and build. But he's different somehow. The doctor hasn't got flying in his bones."

"I bet you caught a monarch today."

Miss Charlemaigne's eyes are naked. Unveiled. At this moment, Cora sees, Miss Charlemaigne has no interest in butterflies. "Take that face and make it a little older. A girl's face." Miss Charlemaigne pulls her gaze from the doctors' son, whispers to the grass, "Oh my, yes."

Cora backs away, embarrassed.

"Cora, just ignore a silly woman's rantings. He's a fine-looking boy is all. There's something wonderfully reckless about him, something entirely unlike the good doctor." And Miss Charlemaigne shuffles toward the graveyard gates. She stops, twirls her butterfly net against her shoulder. Waits until she is certain she has Cora's attention.

"Here's a thing," she says. "An interesting tidbit about butterflies. Male butterflies. In flight, you see, they rub their back legs together. Just a simple rubbing action. This releases an aphrodisiac. You know what that is, yes? This aphrodisiac makes the female swoon. Just that easy. She gets sleepy. Or in more extreme situations it knocks her out."

"Oh." Cora isn't sure where this is leading.

"Smells like vanilla," says Miss Charlemaigne, shaking her killing jar. She stops and looks at the orange butterfly. "Some say apples. Now here's a thought. Just what do you think would happen if thousands of those males rubbed their legs together all at once? Ha! Imagine."

And Miss Charlemaigne turns to the bush, carrying her sorrow over her shoulder with her net.

## A Fine Daughter

~

Cora, her face deep within the darkness of her nightie, knows that Fran, still leaning against the door, is carefully choosing her words. But Cora wants to stay where the light is mottled, where Flury shifts like a warm wind. His name. Flury. She whispers to the recesses of her body, Flury. Feels the fluttering of his name against her skin. Flury.

And it was Miss Charlemaigne, thinks Cora, who told Fran.

Cora feels Fran's weight as she sits beside her. Feels cool air on her neck as Fran lifts her hair and begins to run her fingers down her spine. Cora knows what Fran, in her conical bra and solid girdle, is steeling herself to say. Knows that she, Cora, is living proof of a warning unheeded.

*Fran*

FRAN, sitting beside Cora, removes the gloves she wears to protect her hose. She looks at Cora with her head tucked into the neck of her nightie like a turtle. Fran thinks of the life within that flannel, her daughter on that magical ledge between childhood and adulthood. Fran lifts a hand to her daughter's neck, lifts the hair from her back and runs her fingers down her spine just as she did the first time she held her. That wet and naked body. Fran looks at Cora, licks her lips, feels awkward, but forces words from her mouth. "There are consequences, Cora, of certain behaviors."

Now if that doesn't sound limp, thinks Fran, what does? She tries again. "On Little Cypress Hill, Cora, you could get into trouble. You could meet someone."

Cora's head emerges from her nightie. "I figured out why she hangs around me so much. Why Miss Charlemaigne's always trying to tie bows in my hair. She wants to know who my father is. That's why she looks at me like that."

Fran takes a breath, begins to stop her daughter, but here, she thinks, is a moment's reprieve. Cora can stall for both of them. "Oh," says Fran, "really?"

"Definitely. She tells me all this stuff about butterflies, sits her big fat bum beside—"

"Cora!"

"She sits beside me on the McLellan stone and tells me things that are interesting just so I'll get all relaxed and slip out some information about my father. She may as well whisper, 'Who's your daddy?' the way she looks at me."

"I wouldn't be so sure about that, Cora."

"I'm positive. She's never squinted at you like that, Mom. I ought to know. She wants to throw her butterfly net over me and take me home. She wants to put me to sleep or something. Knock me out with the ether she uses on her butterflies. She wants to dissect me because she thinks she'll find my father inside my shoulder blades. Or that if she pops out my eyeball she'll find a picture of him, you know, in the inside of my eyesocket."

"Good god, Cora, what next? I think you're barking up the wrong tree. Entirely. Miss Charlemaigne couldn't give two hoots about your father. I think she's drawn to you because you're—"

"Know what?" Cora pulls her legs out from her nightie.

"What?"

"I finally told her. I got tired of her, so I up and told her."

"Well, good for you."

"It was like this. Miss Charlemagne's sitting beside me on the McLellan stone. And the whole time she's talking, I'm rubbing the letters on the stone with my fingers. She goes on about the senses of butterflies. She's telling me how butterflies can see colors that we don't even know exist, how they can see a whole spectrum beyond our blue. So I'm working on seeing past blue, staring at the sky and believing that really I'm getting beyond the ultraviolet region, when she gets her hands in my hair again. You know. She's always got that pink ribbon in her pockets, and she'll do anything to get me to sit still so she can tie a bow. Just when

I'm starting to see what maybe happens after blue. So I figure it's time to give her what she wants. Figure I'll just tell her point-blank so she can stop trying to catch me off guard."

Fran's got to get moving. She can't sit here all morning listening to Cora. So she moves into the bathroom, picks up her face cream and returns to the bed.

"I lift my finger from where I've been rubbing the stone and lick it. I trace the McLellan name on the stone again. 'My father's dead,' I tell Miss Charlemaigne. 'He died before I was born.' She drops her hands from my hair and looks at me with her mouth open wide. So I tell her the story."

"Oh," says Fran, rubbing her Nivea in a slow circle beneath her eye. "Now, what story would that be?"

"Well, you're the one who told me. It was his appendix that killed him."

"I've never told you any such thing."

"Well, I told Miss Charlemaigne you did. I told her how one night, just before I was born, my father got a bad pain in his stomach. I told her you both figured the pain was on account of your pregnancy. You thought he was having sympathy pains. Some men do that, you know. Some men even get big in the belly right along with their wives. This happens when two people are very much in love. And you and my father, I told Miss Charlemaigne, were very much in love."

"I see." Fran dips her finger into the cream again. "So it was his appendix giving him pain. Not sympathy."

"Exactly. But you didn't know this, and you went to a movie to forget about his cramp, which kept getting worse."

"That wasn't very smart of us."

"No, but you didn't know better. Besides, *Casablanca* was playing and you both knew once I was born you'd have no chance for movie-going, what with my diapers and feeding and what have you."

"What did Miss Charlemaigne have to say about our poor judgment?"

"Not much. She just sat with her butterfly net over her shoulder and her killing jar between her legs and mostly kept quiet while I talked. She said, 'How sad,' when I got to the death of my father."

"I imagine she did." Fran, finished with the cream, replaces the lid and moves into the bathroom. In the mirror she can see Cora behind her. "So when does he die?"

"When Ilsa gets on the airplane to fly out of Casablanca. Just as she takes off, when Rick Blaine rips out his heart knowing he'll never see her again, my father groans. Slumps forward just as the plane takes off. And you, Mom, let loose your floodgates and weep for Rick and Ilsa. And right then, with the whole audience weeping, with you sobbing into your hands, my father dies."

Fran, leaning toward the mirror, closes one eye and brushes the lid with grey powder. "That's pretty maudlin."

"Maybe. But it suits you to be crying in a dark theater, crying for two lovers, when right beside you, the only man you've ever loved sits green and sick, poisoned by a burst appendix."

"Thanks."

"When you discover him dead, and your tears become tears for him, and for me, your unborn daughter, you decide right then, in that very movie house, to leave town. You could never live again in the cozy house you shared with him, could never close the green curtains with tomatoes on them or sleep without him in the bed with the electric blanket you got for a wedding present. You knew you could never again walk down the street of your hometown without thinking of his warm hand in yours."

"Good heavens, Cora. Poor Miss Charlemaigne having to listen to that."

"That's how we ended up here in Little Cypress, I told her. I told her how you carried my father out of that movie house sobbing, carried him to the train station. You got a doctor to sign the death certificate and had his body sent here by train. You followed two days later."

"That's some story, Cora." Fran turns from the mirror, looks along the floor for her hose. She's distracted.

"It was Miss Charlemaigne who figured out we were sitting on his gravestone. I kept my fingers busy tracing the McLellan name on the stone, over and over, until finally she looked at my fingers and her hand shot up to her mouth and she said, 'He's buried here? Right here?' I patted the stone. 'You bet,' I said."

"Cora, where are my gloves? I know I had them a minute ago."

Cora leans across the bed, plucks Fran's white cotton gloves from the top of the quilt. "Here," she says. "I think Miss Charlemaigne was uncomfortable sitting on him. She wiggled like a caterpillar on a hot leaf, so then I told her about the eggplants."

"The what?"

"Eggplants. I've been reading about them to the old lady."

"I see." Fran reaches for her gloves.

Cora takes her hair, twists it into the nape of her neck, tucks it into her nightie. "I told her you can't talk about him. I told her how you're fine until something reminds you of him. Like me and eggplants."

"What?" shouts Fran, half-snorting, her head tossed back and her mouth wide open.

Cora smiles at her. "Yeah. I told her how my eyes are just like his. And my hands. I'm so like him, I told her, my mother sometimes can't stand looking at me."

"A little too close, Cora. A little too close." It is true, thinks Fran. Blonde hair, skin almost translucent. Cucumber thin. Long limbs, her legs at seventeen still horsey. Just like the man who fathered her. Fran and Cora share only the birthmark, the brown stain on their right buttock.

"And you can't stand looking at eggplants either, I told her. That's when she reached down to pick up her stupid box."

"She must have been fed up with your babble."

"No. It turns out she was preparing a gift for me. Anyway, I told her while she fiddled with her killing jar that my father grew eggplants. He had a weakness for growing things. So one year he planted eggplants in the kitchen. Twenty varieties. Little round things and big ones and all the shades including white.

"But then Miss Charlemaigne manages to open that killing jar of hers. Really, right when I'm into telling her how the skin of an eggplant is as smooth as the belly of a fish, she opens her net over the jar and pushes an orange butterfly into it. It's the second one she's caught in as many days. I watched its wings hit the glass. 'Go on,' she says. The butterfly's slowing down. It flutters. A few seconds later a smaller flutter. Then, it does this kind of dance. A few quick short steps. Slow-slow, quick-quick, slow. Then it's gone.

"I turned to look right at her. She's ruined my day and my story. 'I'm making a gift for you,' she says. 'Remember the painted lady I told you about? Here's one for you to keep.' Then she lifts the dead butterfly out of the jar with tweezers. 'Oh, my pretty one,' she says and tries to hand it to me."

Women and butterflies, thinks Fran. Ether. If she had been given chloroform or ether to birth Cora, chances are Cora would not be hers today. If Dr. Johnson had been there to administer twilight sleep, thinks Fran, returning to the bathroom, she would have let the doctor lift her baby girl from her arms as she was expected to, would have watched him turn his back and walk from the room with that warm flesh still smelling of her womb.

As it was, there was no ether or chloroform or twilight sleep for Fran, and so she learned the power of—what? Instinct, she thinks, bending to lift her hose from the floor. It's instinct that lets you know when and how to make a baby, how to open your legs and your arms, how to grow one deep in your body. It's instinct that tells you how to birth a baby.

Fran, with her hose collected, sits on the bed beside Cora, puts on her white gloves for what seems like the umpteenth time this morning. She considers how, after the blood from birthing is spilled, how when the fibers are torn and the joints have given, graciously or not, there's something that happens, there's a mountain of feeling that says *I've climbed you. I've been to the top. I had doubts and I faltered. I lost faith maybe for a moment. But I did it.* There's that, but more important, there's a breathing from the inside out. Breathing from a raw untouched place.

And maybe, thinks Fran, this place is instinct. Fran, inside out from birthing, so close to her inside skin that she could hear it breathing, held Cora away from the tardy doctor's hands as he tried to take the baby, held tight to Cora just as her instinct bid her.

Fran watches Cora tie her hair in knots. Considers how if Cora were not hers, Cora would be on the foot of some other woman's bed.

~

A full moon in an indigo sky, thinks Fran, seventeen years ago. She sits at the table looking out the window, Frank's Barbershop below, the red and white pole black and grey in the night, Cora inside her curled and wiggling. She pushes, rolls, thumps. Stretches again and again against the walls of Fran's womb until she finds a hollow, a place where muscle divides right below Fran's navel. Some part of Cora rises to the place where there is only skin, no wall of muscle or band of tendon between her and her mother. What part of the baby, wonders Fran, is this? What bit of the baby's small body that she can feel so perfectly, that she can practically hold between thumb and forefinger? Backbone? No. A toe? Mmmmm. A heel. Yes, decides Fran, she holds her baby's heel. The heel of her baby pushed into thin skin so that Fran, sitting at the open window looking at the moon, can hold this small part of her baby.

And suddenly Fran sees she's not alone. There is still the suffocating fear of birth and the dread of her error being discovered when she returns home. No aunt to visit, but a general store owner kind enough to employ her, give her the excuse of a holiday.

"Oh my baby," Fran whispers in the darkness at the open window, "I've been so alone. But I feel you now. Somehow," she says, "with your heel in my hand, the moon isn't so cold. It's round. Like me. Like us."

And so Fran sits. When the tightening comes, she stands, walks the length of the room, her breath arcing from her body in a slow moan. She sits again at the open window when the pain subsides, contemplating her baby's oh-so-tiny heel. People or things at this moment are, for Fran, meaningless. Thinking of heels under a white moon, she paces until she feels the tightening crack against her spine, feels the pain move to another level, knows her baby-with-the-heel is set to discover the length of a birth canal.

So she calls Dr. Johnson.

"No, you may not speak to the doctor. He's busy. Very busy. He's opening a can of evaporated milk for our screaming baby and then he's going to feed him. All by himself because he knows just how happy it will make the baby."

She hears the doctor shouting at his wife as another tightening rolls across Fran's body. She drops to her knees, her breath funneling from the throat of her pain, the doctor's voice saying, "Hello, hello," the baby wailing in the background, the receiver swaying in front of Fran's hot forehead. The pain leaks away and she retrieves the receiver. "Sorry, doctor. It's Fran. I . . . it must be time."

"Now, just relax, Fran." Doctor Johnson's voice. "Fran, listen, I'll be there soon. Can you walk to the hospital?"

The screaming baby makes it difficult for Fran to hear the doctor. "What did you say?"

"I said call when the pains are closer. They're not close enough yet."

"How close? When should I call again?"

"Fran, don't call. Get walking. I'll meet you at the hospital."

"When?"

Again Fran feels a tightening, starting at her spine, which wraps around her baby, taking the wind from her. Again she is on her knees, the receiver swinging, as the doctor says, "You go now. While you can still walk. I'll be by in a bit."

Between contractions, Fran runs in the night. Runs when she

can, drops to all fours when a contraction hits. Fran moans, aware of nerves she never knew she had.

When Fran arrives at the hospital, a young nurse takes her by the hand, eases the clothes from her body. Dresses her in a crunchy blue hospital gown. Puts her cool hand on Fran's belly, feels the baby lift and churn under the swelling of muscle and tells Fran she hasn't the training to administer ether.

"That's okay," says Fran leaning against the wall of the hospital, her naked back feeling the cool ivory-colored paint. "The doctor will be here. He said he would." Another tightening rolls deep across the ocean of her body, and Fran presses her hot skin to the wall for support.

The nurse listens to Fran, hears the depth of the note inching low and white from Fran's throat and knows that Fran is close to birthing her baby.

"I doubt he'll make it," the nurse tells Fran, who, released from the pressure of her womb, lifts her wet face. "I think you're going to have to do this just as you are."

In that moment Fran gives herself to the baby with the heel, planting all consciousness in her womb. Fran slips into her body.

The nurse tells Fran her name is Mailyn, then, knowing she's involved for the duration, gives Fran her arm to clench. Mailyn moves with Fran in harmony to the moans moving from the cave of Fran's body. Mailyn cannot dispense ether, cannot ease Fran's pain, but can, in the moonlit hospital room, crouch on the floor with Fran and knead with her own hands the rippling muscles that force Cora downward.

Fran squats while Mailyn drops her voice and comforts her by moaning with her. The muscle in Fran's womb pushes down down, forcing air from the hollows of Fran's belly which, as her thighs begin to quake, funnels up her throat in one long wail until there is no air left, only the urgent need to push. To open her legs wide. To let her bones melt to the size of a baby's head.

So it is the nurse and not Dr. Johnson who first sees Cora's head urging through Fran. It is Mailyn who celebrates Cora's crowning. She lifts her fingers to Fran, eases back skin as though working a too-small turtleneck over a head, which, in a panting, is born. After the shoulders have swiveled round and spilled out, Mailyn takes Cora's small body between her hands and lifts her onto Fran's tummy.

Cora on the outside is slippery and white. Is this a leg or an arm? Which wet limb, wonders Fran, beginning to laugh, is she gripping? The heel! Yes, the glorious heel! In the palm of Fran's hand, a heel leading to a leg, which gives way to a thigh, a tummy, a chest. A tiny, mewing, mottled face. Lips fine as a rosebud. A human body in Fran's arms, a baby whole and entirely hers.

Fran laughs with the nurse as Cora's behind lifts to moonlight, and they see Cora's birthmark, the same as Fran's, on the right buttock. Mailyn and Fran laugh for the joy of a baby brought to breath through a night of pain.

The lights flash on. In the brightness Dr. Johnson says, "Need a little light on the subject here." He looks down at Fran. "That baby came fast. Faster than expected from a primipara."

The nurse, still holding Fran's hand, says, "No, she labored most of the night."

"Primiparas are notoriously slow." The doctor leans close to the nurse, says something Fran cannot hear. And Fran, with the wiggling Cora damp in her arms, feels the nurse's hand tighten against her leg.

The doctor shuffles his feet, drops awkwardly to his knees.

He pushes her legs apart. Fran watches as he lowers his head to stare at the place which has just birthed Cora. "You tore," he tells Fran. "You'll need stitches."

But it doesn't matter to Fran that the lights are on and the doctor's head is between her legs, his hand on the cord, pulling the placenta from her womb. It doesn't matter either when he starts to sew, his hand needling Fran's skin. None of it matters because she has Cora in her arms. Cora with a round mouth and wide eyes, her mouth at Fran's nipple.

Mailyn strokes Cora's cheek, her hand on her face so her mouth opens. And Mailyn urges Fran's nipple into Cora's mouth. Cora begins to suck.

None of it matters, not even the doctor's outstretched hands when he says, "I have a nice couple waiting for this baby."

Fran is confused.

"Come now, child. Your plans all along have been to give the baby up."

Fran says nothing, holding Cora closer.

"Please don't be difficult. There is no way you can raise a child on your own."

"I can."

The doctor sits beside Fran as if to make sense of this for her. "If you keep this child, Fran, your life will never be what it could. You're young. You can go back home and no one will ever know this happened."

Fran drops her eyes, can feel the blood on Cora's skin saying no no.

"Fran, it was your plan. Please don't ruin your life because this little baby feels good to hold. She'll grow up and need more than you can give her. Think of your life, Fran. You're a clever girl.

Be reasonable. If you love her you'll stick to your plan. Now, give me the baby."

"No. No. Nononono."

~

The old lady downstairs coughs. Coughs again and again, reminding Fran that she ought to be dressing, not dreaming. "Oh dammit. I've been messing around. I'm behind." And Fran unfurls the nylon up her thigh.

# The Old Lady

THE WIND RATTLES THE OLD LADY'S WINDOWS. She draws her blankets closer to her neck, then reaches for the jar on her bedside table. It is open already. She has been awake for some time now, alone in the darkness, sniffing.

The old lady lowers her nose to the jar, inhales, and the honey-eyed scent of linden blossoms transports her to the days when it was her task to wake her husband.

~

In morning's hush she slips across his warm and sleeping torso. She wraps her still-dreamy thighs about his. There, atop him, she rocks, urging him from sleep. She sways against his chest, breathes the fragrance she worked into his skin last night.

In the evenings her husband's shoulders are tired from lifting boxes of tin cans onto the shelves of their store. Tired, he says, from emptying flour and rice into bins. So she takes blossoms from the linden tree which shades the back courtyard, pulverizes them into a paste with buttermilk and honey. Before he sleeps she massages the mixture into his shoulders, easing the work of the day from his body.

In the morning, as she lifts her hips over his, and he eases into her, it is the linden blossom she smells. Honey and buttermilk wrap the thin skin of their bodies together as they begin to move. Their pleasure builds, their breath like hot gusts of wind rushing at each other. Finally she drops her forehead to his chest. Their breathing slows. "You awake yet?" she asks.

~

The old lady lifts her head to the jar. Shuts out the sound of the wind and the knowledge of her narrow bed. She inhales love, rides Gorkey, the warm undertow of honey and buttermilk lapping between her thighs. The old lady sniffs again and again until finally the reckless scent makes her cough. Her cough wakes her son. Her cough lets Fran and Cora know morning has truly arrived.

The old lady opens her eyes to an empty room and, as she does every morning, acknowledges her final task. She must die so her son will know this joy. Then the old lady places the lid on the jar and, rolling onto her side, pushes the jar beneath her bed. She listens to the wind and laughs out loud. Cora, she thinks. Lovely Cora. Wind and kites. "If his father had him flying kites, you would have met him," she'd said to Cora. But that wasn't how she knew. No. The answer lay in Cora's breath. As his name was mentioned, as Winnie said "Flury," Cora gulped air, held it in her lungs as though she anticipated the pleasure of linden blossom fragrance.

*Fran*

FRAN LEANS FORWARD, grasps her garter, pulls it to the heavy top of her nylon and imagines Gorkey waking below. She slips the plastic nub below the nylon's surface, guides the metal clasp over top and thinks of the fingers on Gorkey's left hand. She sees how in the sleepy darkness his thumbnail sails across the white of his collarbone, moves in an arc across his hairless chest. Fran's fingers grasp the garter behind her thigh. He'll sit on the edge of his bed, wiggle his long toes against the cool of the yellow linoleum and listen, she knows, for the hushed voices above. Thinking of Gorkey on the edge of his bed listening for her voice, she begins to sing, "With some . . . one like you . . . a pal good and true. . . ." Fran whirls the nylon over her other foot, lifts her voice against the wind and sings to Gorkey as he, in darkness, wiggles his toes. "I'd like to leave it all be . . . hind and go and find . . ."

"Would you stop that."

"What?"

"It's embarrassing."

"Embarrassing who? There's no one here but you and me, girl."

"You look stupid."

"I do?" Fran, with one nylon on, the other halfway up her thick leg, stands.

"Yeah. You look silly, you know, with those white gloves on, as though you're going to some cocktail party in your bra and girdle."

"Oh, but I am. I'm having a special kind of party, Cora. One where it really doesn't matter if you're wearing your little Peter Pan collar or your oh-so-sweet A-line."

Fran lifts a leg to her daughter, points her toe, knowing, as she brings her hands to her cheeks, just how ample and dimpled she is. Knows, with the white skin ballooning from the elastic pinch of her girdle and the dampness shining between her breasts, that she ought, with her hair wrapped in toilet paper in an attempt to maintain her hairdo, to feel somewhat ashamed. To be standing here in the bold light looking positively ridiculous.

She looks at her thick ankle and the nylon which pools about it, then lifts her eyes to Cora. "The thing is," she says quietly, "I don't feel stupid. Or silly. Remember 'The Emperor's New Clothes'? Hmmmm? Remember his naked parade?" Fran pulls in her ample tummy, arcs her white-gloved hand across her shoulder to pull a cape of crimson velvet from the air. Then, as though drawn by a golden thread, Fran drifts across the room, her cape fluttering vermilion after her. She turns to Cora and lifts an eyebrow. The wind roars applause. Fran raises a hand. The wind drops. And in the silence Fran stands, the brown birthmark on her buttock showing through the beige of her girdle, two garters undone and ringing like bells against her monarch thigh.

"If I teach you nothing else, Cora, I want you to understand that we are magnificent. You and me, Cora. We're beautiful." Fran bends to pull at the nylon about her ankle and lifts her face. "This is important, Cora. Always keep the emperor in mind. I don't have to look like Winnie McRae or the doctor's wife. You don't have to look like the girls with their Hula-Hoops who hang around the storefront. No. We're living our own party, and it's not a bad one either. Not at all."

Downstairs the old lady coughs again. "Double damn," says Fran and turns from the bold sun, the wind, to get dressed. She moves across the room to their wardrobe, opens the dark wooden door, lifts out her skirt.

"What is it about this wind?" Fran murmurs, trying to do up the last two garters. Something in the wind making her—what? she wonders, resisting her desire to look longingly at Cora, making her sentimental about Cora. The wind whispering that change is imminent, that mornings of Cora curled like a child in her nightie, of saying Fran looks silly and stupid, are passing. The sweet wind, the wind she can almost taste, making Fran ache for Cora, making her want the right to stroke the tender hair at the nape of Cora's neck forever. Reminding Fran that her task this morning is to warn Cora, suggest that Cora consider what can come of a day on Little Cypress Hill.

Cora is flat on the floor now, her ear pressed to the crack in the floorboard.

"Cora, get up."

"She's coughing more. There's a crackle in her cough. It sounds worse, Mom. Worse than usual."

"Gorkey hates to get the doctor, but if she's worse, perhaps it's time."

"Maybe," says Cora lifting her head to Fran, "she needs to sleep today. Maybe I shouldn't read to her." Cora stands, bends to the hem of her nightie, lifts it up and over her head, her young body like a river in the white room. Cora opens a drawer, lifts out panties, a summer dress. Cora glides, in a liquid movement, into her dress. "Think I'll go up Little Cypress."

Fran looks down at the button on her skirt. Stares at it. Consequences, she thinks, an afternoon on Little Cypress has its consequences.

Fran opens her mouth. "Cora," she says, then pauses, seeing her consequence in sunlight, arms lifted to tie a satin ribbon around her hair. Consequence. Wrong word, thinks Fran.

Fran, still partially dressed, pulls out a chair by the window and sits. Let the day roll on, she thinks, let the sun get in there and eat the day right up. But leave me here, she thinks, with my daughter. Let the day happen without me. Let the women buy potatoes and dishwashing liquid and the men their newspapers, but leave me to sit here with my daughter.

"Why the hell are you sitting down, Mom. You'll be late for work."

Fran shrugs. "I'm enjoying you, that's all."

"Really. You're crazy."

## Cora

FRAN IS STARING AGAIN, thinks Cora, looking at her as though she is a melting snowman or a cloud emptying itself of rain. *I am here*, Cora wants to tell her, *very much here. I'm not disappearing.* Cora puts a hand on Fran's arm and says "Come on, Franny. You've got to get moving."

Fran murmurs "mmmphhhh" as she lifts from the chair. "You're right. I'm a yo-yo."

Cora stands behind Fran in the growing light, brings her hands to Fran's skirt and twists it around to her back. "A dip."

"A nosebleed," says Fran, pulling in her tummy.

"Wanna loose ten ugly pounds?" Cora asks, pushing the button through the hole, touching her mother's fat-lady damp skin with her knuckles. Briefly she bends her forehead to touch the space between Fran's shoulders.

"Sure," says Fran.

"Cut off your head!"

"Har-dee har har," says Fran, just like the boys outside Gorkey's.

Cora watches her mother lift her arms to put on her blouse. Outside the awning thunders as the wind hits it. Fran rushes to the bathroom to douse her toothbrush in the box of baking soda.

Cora presses her cheek against the window's cool glass. The fragrance of ripe apples. Cora wants to run, wants to feel the full thrust of her legs. She wants to stand astride the McLellan stone with the wind lifting skin layer by layer. Here, with her nose to the window, Cora realizes she wants to know the feel of his hands, wants to abandon her heart to hands familiar with the wind.

Cora backs away from the window. Shakes her head.

Frank appears on the street below. He is early. Cora watches as he rounds the corner to his shop. She waits for him to open his barbershop door, but instead he sticks a large handwritten note onto the glass. The wind tears at the note, spins the paper out onto the street. Frank runs after it, stops the frantic dance with his toe. He returns with his note, opens his door and gingerly tucks the paper into the frame before shutting the door. He bends over, making certain the note can be read. As Frank turns away, Cora squints to read what he's written. Though she can't read the finer hand, she can decipher a large CLOSED printed with a bold hand. Frank swaggers up the street and Cora thinks, watching the wind churn his white shirt like reckless clouds, how she's never known Frank's Barbershop to be closed on a Saturday morning. Never, not once.

Cora turns to watch Fran. The water runs but her toothbrush is stilled. She's dreaming, distracted from warning Cora about the kite flyer.

Cora closes her eyes, trying to recall the morning. There's something she's missed, some nuance of Fran's she's oblivious to. Fran's been hesitant. Wanting to warn but unable to.

Cora opens her eyes to the rich texture of peeling paint on the windowsill. Repeats Fran's words: *Might be a good day for flying a kite. It's nice up there, isn't it, when the wind's big?* That was it, wasn't it? That was what she'd said. *And you feel like you can see forever.*

"Mom?" Cora drifts across their room to Fran and turns off the running water. "Mom," she says, taking the wet toothbrush from her hand, "what did you say about flying kites?"

"I don't know. What did I say?"

"You said it was nice up there."

"It is."

Cora tries to recall her mother ever having been up Little Cypress Hill. She's never picnicked up there, never climbed the hill for her Sunday stroll. Fran, with her heavy thighs and long hours, is strictly a Main Street woman.

"How," asks Cora, "do you know what it's like to fly kites up Little Cypress?"

Fran takes the toothbrush from Cora's hand, dabs it in the baking soda box again. "I never said I was up there flying kites."

Cora stares at her blankly. Then shrugs, leans over to turn the tap back on.

Fran smiles and turns the tap off. "Paper birds," she says, "fly too, you know." Then she starts to laugh.

*Fran*

FRAN STICKS THE TOOTHBRUSH into her mouth to quiet herself down. She was drawn to the town by the size of the hill, but stayed because a man whose hands knew the shape of flight had touched her. She stayed all the long summer afternoon and into the evening with a man whose left thumbnail curled perfectly about her nipple.

He told her he wanted to fly.

"We make what we desire," she said to him, watching one of his birds sail across the sky.

So they made Cora.

~

The first time Fran touched Gorkey was almost eighteen years ago, the two of them on Little Cypress Hill, Gorkey making birds. He was up there with a stack of catalogues, just sitting, humming, with the sun on his back.

The view makes Fran, who is from another town, feel big as the hill itself. She stands behind him, warm and out of breath, looking at the tiny houses below, at the women in their backyards hanging laundry, sheets smaller than facecloths. She feels as if her legs are as long as the hill is tall and this tiny world is hers.

She lifts a hand, uses her forefinger to draw the gully beside the railroad tracks. Pushes the earth aside and pats it down to make Main Street running straight out from the hill. She imagines placing little houses, one and then another, side by side to make a neighborhood. Then a Texaco gas station, a coffee shop, a barbershop and the general store with a maroon awning and red door. In the backyards small figures of women come to life, hanging washing on their lines.

In the sky, wheeling over the town, are speckles of flight. Birds. She watches one curve through the air above the town and climb toward her. It lands on the ground close to the young man.

He turns to her and says, "I'm making birds," as if, thinks Fran, to say, *You do the gullies, the neighborhoods and the roads—I'll do the birds.*

So she sits beside him and they share the town, both of them big as the hill. He lifts one of the catalogues from between his legs. "Pick a picture," he says.

"Sure." So she licks her middle finger, turns the pages of the catalogue. Bachelor buttons, wallflower, anemone.

"You must have come up the back."

"What?"

"Of the hill. If you'd come up the front I would have seen you."

"Yeah, I guess. It's a high hill."

"Highest in a long ways. Highest hill this side of the Cypress Hills."

"I always wanted to get up here. You can see this hill from my back window. Looks like a mole on the face. It took leaving at five in the morning to get here. Early, right? But that's when I woke up with something saying head for the hill instead of all the other directions I generally walk. So I did. When there's a voice inside me talking, I generally listen."

"Oh."

She turns a few more pages of the catalogue and lifts her head to the view. "It's some hill."

"You mean you walked here? You've been walking since 5:00 A.M. to get here?"

"Yeah, sure. I like walking."

"You do this all the time? Where're you from, anyway?"

"I walk Saturdays. All day. I'm from Stavely. You can't see it from this side. Round back you can." Then pointing down to his town, she says, "Named after the Cypress Hills?"

"Wasn't always called Little Cypress. I like its old name better."

"Oh?"

"Smith. Used to be Smith."

"Smith? Boring."

He shrugs. Turns his head to look over his shoulder toward the graveyard. "You going to pick a picture?"

"Sure." And she begins to turn the pages of the catalogue again.

"Smith's not such a dry name if you know the story."

"Tell me."

He brings both his hands together over his knees, straightens out his pile of catalogues. "There was once a couple who walked aimlessly down the railway track. The woman saw the hill and said it was time to stop. So they stopped. It's a sad story. You still want to hear it?"

"Sure." She picks a yellow begonia blossom, tears out the picture and says, "How about this?" and hands it to him after reading, "The begonia is a valuable garden plant because it prefers the shade, where it flowers freely."

He takes the torn paper and bends his body protectively as if she has handed him something rare and delicate. Fran, with her knees drawn to her chest, pulls her eyes from the town below. She watches, riveted, as the young man twists the paper this way and folds to the left, watches as he holds his breath, unfurls his thumbnail and slices the excess paper from what is now a canary's wing.

He holds the small bird toward the sky. It trembles against the wind. Finally he lets go, lets the wind breathe life into the small bird. The canary rises, begins to fly, circling the town, golden as the sun. Round and round it flies, over the town with the tiny women hanging laundry in their backyards, casting a shadow smaller than a needlepoint on the late September grass.

"They settle here. The lady gives birth to a daughter," says the man, "but the gypsy, lacking heart, sells it to some coyotes for iron so he can continue to work as a blacksmith. The woman weeps as the baby is taken away. Eventually the heartbroken woman goes mad, wondering about her daughter with the coyotes."

"You sure it's coyotes that raise the child? Doesn't sound right."

"Why not? Anyway, the grief of separation finally kills her. The gypsy lady dies and the gypsy has to bury her.

"So he carries her up this hill, and, feeling remorse, wishing forgiveness, buries her where she can see all. Here she can keep watch over her child."

"That's good. I mean, it's a good place to put her."

"I guess so. Anyway, the blacksmith used the iron he got from the coyotes to forge the graveyard gates. They're over there. You may have noticed them. The gypsy created them, but in the process, he got a bit of iron lodged in his throat and could no longer talk. He was silenced, you see, by what he'd received in place of the child. So he was silent the rest of his days. Lonely too. When he died, he left only three iron graveyard gates and the town named for his trade: Smith."

"Mmmm. You think it's true?"

"Not likely. But it's interesting. I mean, no one knows how the gates got here."

"I believe it," she says. "The story. That kind of thing happens."

He rubs his knee and looks at her. "Maybe," he says, "it was fairies that looked after the child. Not coyotes. Coyotes doesn't sound right, does it?"

She shrugs. Keeps her mouth tight, tries not to laugh, but finally can't help it. "No," she says, "coyotes doesn't sound right." She wipes her eyes, clears her throat. "So what happened to the name? Smith?"

"The hobos going through on the train started calling the town Little Cypress. Most of them had seen the Cypress Hills, going back and forth the way they did, and the important people in the town didn't like the association with the gypsy. Didn't like the story, or so my father said. To help people forget, they renamed the town. Called it Little Cypress."

"Mmm. Who would do that?"

"The mayor for one. The doctor's father, back when he was the mayor."

"And you? Who are you?"

"What?"

"Your name. What's your name?"

"Oh." He puts back his head and laughs. "One thing's for sure, I'm not the doctor or the mayor. Mine's a funny name. No one knows it really, because they call me Gorkey. The store's Gorkey's General. They called my father Gorkey."

"Gorkey?"

"Yeah. Though the name's Anosia."

"Anosia. That's okay. Nice." Fran looks down to the outskirts of town. Follows the railway track to the train station and from the station up Main to Gorkey's maroon awning.

"You work there?"

"Mmmmm. Always have. So tell me about this walking thing you do."

"Saturdays, I pick a direction, pack my lunch and go."

Gorkey looks at her with his mouth open. "I'd like that," he says. He moves his hand to the catalogue she holds, takes it from her, and in one quick movement, tears a page from the order section. He bends his head to his work, strokes the feathers of his creation while he folds and presses. "Thing is, I've got work in the store. Saturdays especially. But if I thought about it, there's nothing stopping me from walking Sundays."

"What's it like working there? In the general store?" She watches as he looks down the hill to the store. He takes longer to answer than she expects.

At last he blinks and says, "The big thing is the light. It's dark. Shady in there." Gorkey looks again at his creation, cups his palm over the bird, then lifts it until the wind ruffles its feathers, and in a grey swoop the bird is up and off, growing small in the sky's immensity.

They watch the bird drift above the town, flicker on an updraft.

"What I'd like most," says Gorkey, "is to fly."

Fran watches the bird and considers Gorkey's art. "I guess," says Fran, "we make what we desire."

Months later, walking the hot June railway track, her brown loafers sticky with sweat, Fran thinks of having said *we make what we desire* and laughs out loud. As if, she thinks, either of us made this baby because we desired one.

Fran turns from the track, steps onto Main Street in the silence of the hot day. One by one the people of Little Cypress stop what they are doing to watch her. She continues her walk, wraps her hands around her large tummy and whispers the story of the emperor's new clothes to herself.

This, she says, is my parade.

Fran, moving up Main Street, considers again the words that got her here. "We make what we desire," she said to Gorkey. And he turned to her then and took hold of her arm, his skin hot.

Hot, thinks Fran touching the crackled red paint of the front door of Gorkey's General, his body hot as this paint. A heat which moved along her arm and into her spine, moved across her chest with the white force of lightning. Cracking her wide open, thinks Fran, pulling at the door, so that the voice within became a plumb line to the heart. Yes! Yes!

Fran opens the door to the darkness of Gorkey's and recalls how, when asked about the store, he'd told her, "It's dark," he'd said. "Shady." And swimming into the dimness of the store, the cool lifting from the hardwood, her feet relieved already, Fran recalls how Gorkey had taken her begonia and given it flight.

Fran pauses then, stops in the dingy light of Gorkey's General and believes for a moment that she is mad. As if there can be flight from such a place. As if blossoming can happen here. Run, she tells herself. But the baby shifts in the darkness of her belly and she cannot think of any direction except forward. Fran holds the baby's movement in the palm of her hand. "I'll work here," she tells Gorkey as he moves toward her in the calm of the store's dappled light.

~

Fran, almost eighteen years later, laughs. She swings her ample hip against Cora. Slowly she brings her hands to Cora's face. Fran looks the consequence of an afternoon on Little Cypress in the eye.

## *Mari*

MARI CURVES THE PALMS of her hands around her stargazer lily. Squatting in her garden she protects her plant from the wind. She knows she can't stay like this all morning, but she can't bear to see how the wind makes the lily bend, how the wind pushes it over until she is certain the stem will snap. Maybe, she tells herself, in a minute or two the wind will die.

But really, she thinks, as she admires the nutmeg dots in the throat of her lily, this is quite pleasant, being out here. Mari lifts her head from her lily to the fullness of her garden. Her snapdragons wheeze and hunch to the earth like old men. The leaves on her poplar show their silver undersides.

Elwood hides behind the poplar. Elwood in a coonskin hat, wielding a six-shooter. Only she's not to call him Elwood anymore. No, she must call him Davy Crockett.

Mari doesn't want to make a mountain out of a molehill, but she misses Elwood. Davy is a far cry from Elwood, and he's not particularly easy to be around either. Too much shouting and gunfire. Mari mourns the loss of her boy. She mourns the way her son slipped on the Davy Crockett costume, making Elwood almost impossible to find.

Once, Mari managed to remove the coonskin. Slowly, without the hat or the guns, Elwood re-emerged. Yes. The night before the baseball game, thinks Mari, hands curved around her lily, Elwood, not Davy, followed the butterfly into the mulberry night.

Mari shifts her weight, enlarges the space between her palms to give her stargazer lily room to breathe and thinks how while she's missing her boy, his father, Howard, applauds the change.

It's all in the photo, all there. Two weeks ago Howard took Elwood by the hand to a baseball game, saying, "This is what you do; a father takes a son to watch baseball."

And when the photo was developed Howard had proof that Elwood finally was functioning in a very ordinary way. He was, after all Howard's hard work, just like every other boy.

~

Howard stands on the front porch holding a photograph toward her as though it's a first-place ribbon. "See," he says. "Look, honey. Look at this. Your son is happy as all get-out. I don't know what you've been moaning about."

"Stop it."

"Well, you've got to admit it. Look here." Howard places the photograph of father and son at a baseball game in her hand. And Mari, seeing two smiling people, wonders why she's making such a big deal out of nothing. In the photo Elwood looks happy. Both of them on their feet, arms up, cheering.

Mari licks her lips and tastes salt. Tries to ignore what she cannot name in the grey and white lines that carve the figure of her son. It isn't the baseball cap, although the absence of the coonskin is a small miracle. "How'd you manage to get the coonskin off his head? And the baseball cap on?"

"Ha! It took some doing. We had a little talk and, you know, he's listening. Learning to listen."

"So what'd you say?" Mari brings her hand to her forehead, shielding her eyes from the sun.

"The truth. Told him at baseball games you wear a baseball cap. Just like when you go to church you wear nice clothes. Your mother, I told him, wears a hat and nice gloves for church. And him wearing that goofy coonskin to a baseball game is the same as if you wore your gardening gloves to church. Simple."

"So what'd he say?"

"Well, he took a little convincing. I told him if you wore gardening gloves to church people would figure you were either a commie or that you had some kind of mental illness. Which would be true if you wore gardening gloves to church. Look Mari, he wore his baseball cap and behaved like every other boy at a baseball game. He ate popcorn and cheered. Why's the hat such a big deal?"

Mari shrugs, thinks of Elwood without his coonskin, a butterfly orange as dawn skimming the air before his outstretched arms. Elwood scooping butterfly scent into his palms.

Howard lifts his hand to Mari's elbow. "Look, I gave him an easy lesson," says Howard. "I told him plain and simple that if he wants to get on in the world, he has to look what others are doing or wearing and do or wear it. Damn fine advice if you ask me."

"Of course," says Mari and looks at the photo quickly as though she's intent on catching a wood nymph. But it is no good. In the black-and-white photo are two baseball fans, a boy and his father. Could be any boy. Larry, Ralph, Sam.

Mari drops the photo into her handbag and, crossing her arms over her belly, walks across her yard. She sits on the grass, back against the poplar, and, looking up at a sky so blue there is no distance, she contemplates Elwood without coonskin. Is he different? Or is she only imagining his ability to hear the creak of a butterfly wing? Mari closes her eyes, recalls Davy/Elwood crashing through the weak branches of the cotoneaster hedge.

~

"For crying out loud, Elwood, you'll kill the hedge."

No response, just a gun in the face.

"Cut that out, please. Put the gun away."

"Davy," he says, one eye closed, the other trained on her. "Call me Davy."

"All right. Davy. Gather up your guns, Davy. The day's done."

"Not on your life, lady. I'm not finished with the bad guys out back."

"Yes you are. It'll soon be dark. And it's getting cold. Past your bedtime."

Davy steps closer to her, says in a stern but gentle voice, "In a minute. Like I said," and he leans nearer yet, looking her dead in the eye, "I'm not done."

Mari lifts her hand to Davy's head, plucks off his coonskin, rubs his fine hair. "You've done all you're doing today, young man."

Davy's hand flies to his head, his eyes hot. "My hat. Give me my hat."

Mari lifts her thigh, tucks the coonskin under her leg.

"Now!" he shouts. And like a wild thing he begins to claw at her leg.

"Settle down," says Mari. Then, more loudly, "Stop that right now!" He brings both hands to his head, and with flat palms he begins to rub his skull, frantically at first and then, like a toy whose battery is running low, more slowly. He dips his head to her chest, still rubbing, until gradually he rests his upper body on hers. She wraps her arms about him, pulls him to her lap, slowly, gently rubs his head where he left off. Over and over, while the summer sky eases from lemon to rose.

Mari sits with Elwood on her lap for a long time. She keeps trying to make herself rise, knows she ought to get him into the house and into the bath, but stalls. Happy with her son on her lap, the two of them sit quietly until a butterfly flutters through the apricot dusk.

"It's just the color of setting sun, isn't it, Elwood? Isn't it just the very color?"

Elwood nods.

They watch it tumble, wings singed ochre.

And then Elwood pulls from her lap, follows the butterfly through the evening air. Mari pulls her legs to her chest to warm herself against the cool as the butterfly alights on the crab-apple tree, then lifts and flutters off.

Elwood tilts his head. Follows. The butterfly's fiery wings, surreal against the purple twilight, spark across the yard. Wings open and glowing, it pauses on the edge of the birdbath. And Mari realizes, watching Elwood, watching the way he tilts his head, that he hears something, hears a fine sound, which somehow belongs to the butterfly, disappearing into darkness and re-emerging at the back of the garden by the tall sunflowers.

Mari stretches forward, wanting to see Elwood better. Through the deep dusk she watches how, as the butterfly takes flight, Elwood cups air in his hands, brings the butterfly scent to his nose and sniffs.

The butterfly sinks into the darkness, but Elwood continues

to scoop air like water. "Smell, Mommy, smell," he says, bringing handfuls of scorched perfume to her nose.

"Mmmmmm," she says, her face in his hands. She thinks, as she inhales the dampness of his palms and the little boy dirt that lives there, what a gift, what a gift. She wonders, does he hear a song in the churning of the butterfly's tiny wings? Can he hear its orange-sherbet humming? If Mari were to pull him onto her lap and press her ears to his almost transparent temples, would she hear his internal whisperings too?

~

Mari in the wind, on her knees before her lily, shakes her head hard to get her windblown hair out of her eyes without lifting her hands from her stargazer. She shakes her head and realizes she's smiling at the memory of Elwood's earnest palms. His gift to her, a butterfly's scent.

Good heavens, thinks Mari, what next? Maybe she is worrying about Elwood too much. Perhaps it was lack of sleep that led her into gossip with Winnie at the back of Gorkey's. Or maybe she'd been gardening too long in the heat. At any rate some kind of unclear thinking took Mari to the back of Gorkey's. There, among the detergents and Chore Boys, she showed the photo of Elwood at the game to Winnie. Mari was surprised at her own gall, amazed at Winnie's response. Winnie touched the photograph of her boy, ran her fingers over the image of Elwood like she was reading Braille, her eyes sad.

~

Winnie, with her shopping lists and pearls, is hard for Mari to take. Her blouse brittle. Winnie's black-and-white laundry floats on lines above her well-manicured lawn every single Saturday morning before nine. She feeds her family, Frank, the barber, and her two girls, Sue and Jane, two vegetables, always different colors, and a portion of meat every night at six on the button. So say the women.

Mari is well aware of Winnie's large following, knows that it's Winnie who sets the pace. Ah, to have that "Winnie look," to be as fresh as slim as cheerful, to be as red-headed and buxom. To have daughters who, like Winnie's, never have a hole in the big toe of the right sock curled up and hidden inside a shoe, who never wear pajama tops instead of undershirts.

But Mari is happy in her garden. She prefers to stay among her sunflowers and lilies. She would rather plump earth around the base of her pansies on Tuesday mornings than share conversation and coffee with the other women in Winnie's backyard. Give her Elwood humming and the thick scent of honeysuckle. There isn't much she misses about those coffee mornings.

Except Winnie's hands. Winnie's hands are the throats of stargazer lilies. They have the same creamy smoothness, their freckles, nutmeg dots. Winnie's hands, startling in their private beauty.

Which is why, when Mari hears Winnie's voice in Gorkey's crying out to Fran, "Oh my stars, what a lovely morning!" Mari's eyes slip immediately to the earthen patterns of her own hands.

Despite her gardening gloves, Mari's fingers are stained with dirt. So when Mari hears Winnie's cheerful greeting, she begins pushing back the cuticle of her baby finger with her thumb without meaning to. She loosens a tiny nugget of earth as Fran replies, "Yes, it's a nice day."

Mari rolls the earth between thumb and forefinger, presses it to the hip of her tulip-patterned house dress and looks up just as

Winnie's shopping cart turns into her aisle. Winnie speeds toward her, swift as a clean iron on linen. "Good heavens," she sings, stopping in front of Mari, "I haven't seen you in ages."

Mari feels the breeze Winnie stirs up rushing toward her. She believes for a brief moment she can smell Saturday morning soap swimming from the depths of Winnie's impeccable white blouse. Mari lifts her hands, wanting for a crazy moment to pluck the freshness. "Why, hello, Winnie," she says and drops her hands.

"Can you believe the price of the new potatoes? Honestly! How are you?"

"Oh, I'm fine. Yes. Thank-you."

"You look great, Mari. You really do."

"I'm tired today. I didn't sleep much last night." Mari puts her hand into the produce beside her, curls her fingers about the roundness of a potato. What is it about Winnie that makes her want to talk, to say, as Winnie's lovely hands sweep across the bar of her shopping cart, *To tell the truth, I was up all night having conversations with Howard. You know, the imaginary ones. All night I sat in our kitchen smoking one du Maurier after another, telling him I don't like how he's made Elwood change. All night I sat with a slipper dangling from my bare foot while he slept wrapped in our new electric blanket. I wanted to find the words to say how I miss Elwood, how I want Elwood, not Davy with his guns and loud voice.*

Of course Mari says none of this. She closes her eyes to Winnie's hands, feels the hardness of the potato and says, "The birds woke me up. They start chirping so early, don't they?"

"I suppose they do. But you look like a million bucks. I'd never guess you were tired." Winnie smiles, her butterfly lips lifting. "And your sweet little boy, Elder, isn't it? How's he?"

"Elwood. He's Elwood and he's . . ." Mari pauses, changing her mind. "Actually he's Davy Crockett."

"Oh! I see. These little boys with their coonskin hats are just the sweetest. More boys wearing coonskins than girls whirling Hula-Hoops nowadays."

"Yes." Mari slows her words. "I guess it's cute. He won't answer unless we call him Davy."

"Children do have lovely imaginations."

"Not really. I mean," says Mari, wanting, with the taste of Winnie's Saturday breeze still in her mouth, to say, *I've lost him, my Elwood, he's gone. The danger of a mimic. You forget your true colors.* But she never completes her sentence. Does not admit to Winnie, though she wants to, that she mourns the boy she once had.

Mari watches Winnie pluck her *Woman's Home Companion* from the top of her vegetables and thinks, as Winnie begins thumbing through the magazine, I'm crazy. Of course a boy cannot cup butterfly perfume, cannot offer hope in his palms. Mari moves her lower lip underneath her top row of teeth and clamps down. Any boy who wears a coonskin becomes Davy and wields guns. Of course. Watching Winnie glance through her *Woman's Home Companion*, Mari appreciates, by degrees that her perspective is skewed.

"I just don't know what I'd do without my *Home Companion*," says Winnie. "I really don't."

Mari watches Winnie with her sleek red hair and her tangerine lips slowly turn the pages of her *Woman's Home Companion*. "Here," she says to Mari, "an article on how to save time in your kitchen. Look at this! They counted Mrs. Ramsey's steps, then rearranged her kitchen. Oh Mari, imagine! Just *that* saved her twenty minutes making dinner. I'll have to get Frank to move *my* stove."

Then Winnie closes her magazine, leans over to drop it on top of her vegetables. And suddenly, to Mari, she is a woman bending into a wild garden, an easiness in her movement, a willingness to embrace the swellings of produce in her cart. Yes, thinks Mari, startled, there is an unexpected calm between Winnie's breasts, beneath her skirts. Winnie is more than she seems.

Mari, watching Winnie bend to the vegetables in her cart, decides that she's not crazy at all. No. Because of something raw and earthy she detects in Winnie, Mari believes Winnie will understand about Elwood. Winnie will know how to get him back.

"He used to be such a gentle boy," says Mari.

"Who?" says Winnie, bending farther into her shopping cart. She pulls out the *Little Cypress News.*

"Elwood. He lay on the grass in my garden for hours at a time." Mari thinks of her love of Elwood's big ears, his thin mouth, his legs. "I believe there are no borders between his senses."

"You what?"

"I mean now, with the coonskin, there are. But before, Winnie, before the coonskin, he didn't have borders. You know. It was like he could smell sounds. I'd pause from gardening, look up to see Elwood sniff the air after a robin had chirped." Mari looks at the new potato still in her hand, puts the nail of her forefinger through the skin. "Or maybe he'd see it." Mari thinks of Elwood seeing a crescent-shaped path of song. "Of course that's what got him into trouble with Howard."

Winnie pulls a tube of lipstick from her handbag. "Naturally. I can imagine it would."

"Howard," Mari tells Winnie, "put up with it until he started taking those articles of Dr. Johnson's seriously."

"Yes, the good doctor," says Winnie. "He's got the answers. Great articles."

Mari shakes her head. When Winnie returns her lipstick to her handbag, Mari swallows the rest of her story.

"The doctor's wonderful, you know," says Winnie. "Insightful. If you have a little problem, just reading his articles can help to iron it out. Let's just see what he's got to say today." She rattles the *Little Cypress News*, begins to read: "Joe Teenager likes his girls natural and not caked with makeup glamor-style. He may whistle at Miss Glamor, but it's Miss Ponytail-from-a-Good-Family he takes to the Junior Prom. Our Joe prefers hiking or kite flying to stalling at the corner grocery. He dislikes curfews, believes the father should earn the living for the family and the mother should keep the home." Winnie lowers the paper, looks at Mari and says, "I was just saying, just the other day in fact, that the doctor would soon write about kite flying."

Mari nods and refuses then to tell Winnie how Howard could tolerate Elwood's ways until he read one of the doctor's articles stressing, "Your child should show his respect by responding to your summons immediately."

Mari does not tell her how Howard hollered at Elwood. "You deaf, son? Would you at least let me know you damned well hear me?" Howard shouting over Elwood where he crouched, ear tilted to the rhubarb.

Howard said to Mari, "The boy can't even hang up his coat."

"His hands get lost when he can't see them," said Mari.

"What the hell?"

"As soon as his hands disappear in the closet, where he can't see them, he doesn't know where they are."

Howard hit the roof. "Now if that isn't just a load of hogwash. That's it. That's the end of that."

He got hard on Elwood. Mari recalled Howard calling her

from the kitchen. She stood before him, her damp hands against her apron, the smell of hamburger, salty and red, frying. "Listen to this," Howard said, snapping the paper straight, his two legs open wide in the crimson chair. "Prior to embarking on the ABCs of school, a child should be well versed in the ABCs of home and personal life. The 'A' in this situation is Articles. A child should be responsible for his own articles. This means placing his baseball cap on the hook by the back door, hanging up his jacket, knowing his baseball glove is in the bin. Recall Ephesians 6:1, which says, 'Children, obey your parents in the Lord: For this is right.'"

Howard looked up at her. "See?" he said. "Stop protecting him. He's already in school. We should expect him to obey us. Time to help him grow up, Mari."

Mari swam through the scent of browning hamburger to her kitchen. She looked at Elwood on the red and white squares of her kitchen floor. He was drawing a picture but had made only one line so far. Mari bent to him, watched him study the line. Saw that even this was impossible for him. The ink from the pen bled into the porous paper.

Elwood had his hands to his ears. Was he deafened, wondered Mari, by the sound of the ink traveling across the paper?

The coat, Mari had intended to tell Winnie, became the goal. Howard would get him to hang up his coat if it was the last thing he did. Every day. Every single day Howard would be there in the evening to say, "Hang up your coat, Elwood. Hang it up. Like this." And he'd show him. Show him over and over. Elwood got so he could do it as long as there were no distractions. But one word, one sound, one flash of a wing from outside the kitchen window and Elwood was gone. He'd see the oboe note from Howard's shifting tie, the lemon of the cat's meow.

*Who knows,* Mari imagines saying to Winnie, *what finally broke him?*

But Mari does know that Howard took him by the shoulders and rattled him. She does know how every single time Elwood's mouth opened in that slow state of awe, Howard would send him to his room.

Mari brings her nail to her mouth, tasting the potato's bitter flesh. Watches Winnie tuck her *Little Cypress News* under her handbag. And though she tries to stop the conversation she's having inside her head, Mari can't. *One night just before dinner, Elwood charged out of his bedroom, where he'd been put by Howard. Only it wasn't Elwood. Really. He marched out of his room wearing the Davy Crockett hat he'd won at a birthday party, hung up his coat and turned on the TV. Insisted on TV dinner that night. Beef in a tinfoil square. Peas in a triangle. The gun blasts and whinnying of horses taking over all the sound from the garden. It's the same every evening now. He won't miss dinner in front of the TV, hasn't missed a single Davy Crockett episode. And you know, Winnie, with the exception of the other night with the butterfly, I've not seen my Elwood.*

Winnie continues to extol the virtues of the good doctor. "Yes, it was just the other day in fact, visiting with Stella, that I said the doctor was sure to write an article against hanging around the storefront. He's subtle, you know. But people get his drift."

And with that Winnie turns to leave. Lifts her beautiful hand to Mari in parting, lifts her hand to wave, but quite suddenly touches Mari, the skin of Winnie's magical palm on her arm confusing her. "I know you're sad," says Winnie, "about your son and husband. They're trying to be the ideal."

Mari stares at Winnie.

Winnie straightens up, her voice again singsongy and cheerful. "It's all there in black and white. In the *Woman's Home Companion*." Winnie clears her voice, closes her eyes. "Listen: 'Ideal married women are gifted with personality and charm as well as the ability to bake, sew, shop, plan menus, iron a shirt, work for the Red Cross, the PTA and their church and keep their husbands happy at the same time.'" Winnie counts off each item, opens her eyes.

"You have that memorized?"

"Of course. I'm almost there. I've just got to work on the happy husband. I'm concerned that I can't, with good conscience, tick off that final point."

"What?"

"Frank. I'm not sure he's happy. Once he's happy, I'll be there."

"Winnie—"

"I don't understand why he wouldn't be happy. He has two lovely daughters and a clean shirt every day. I like him clean."

"Of course," says Mari.

"I have to keep him clean because of the hair. Other people's hair. I can't stand seeing Frank with who-knows-whose hair on him. In fact," Winnie lowers her voice, leaning close to Mari, "I have him change his shirt before we eat."

"You do?" Mari speaks louder than she intends. Fran glances up at her. "You mean he wears two clean shirts a day?"

Winnie nods. "Yes. It's the hair. I can't quit thinking about whose hair—"

"But he wears a barber jacket."

"Oh yes. But even so, I know that bits of someone else's hair still cling to his collar, his shirt cuffs. And if he doesn't change shirts, it ruins dinner for me." Winnie pauses, taps her fingernails on the handle of her shopping cart. "I keep thinking they're eating with us. You know, whoever's hair is all over Frank's shirt. It's like having a personal part of them there—hair, for goodness sake, from their heads, at our dinner table somehow."

"Really?"

Winnie wipes her brow with the back of her hand, breathes, Mari believes, with a hint of exasperation. "I mean, Mari, imagine eating your dinner with a bit of Mr. Rufus clinging to your husband."

"Of course," says Mari.

"Good heavens. The man cleans little children's throw-up off school floors. He's got his head over toilet bowls half the day. He keeps parrots."

Mari nods. "Yes," she says, "I get your drift. I just hadn't thought of it that way."

"Or worse," says Winnie, "Gorkey. Mr. Gorkey. After Frank cuts Gorkey's blond hair—not a grey hair in it, says Frank—I insist that he shower before eating. Really. Gorkey's hair smells like the back rooms. Smells of his aged mother and her years of—" Winnie closes her eyes, sniffs the air, waiting, Mari knows, for the right word. Then she finds it. "Rotting," Winnie says, opening her eyes. "Yes. Gorkey's hair carries the smell of his mother's rotting."

Mari's thumb finds an eye in the potato and works against it, round and round.

"I don't mean to be unkind." Winnie stands up straight. Brings her hand to her mouth and taps her lips with her finger. "I never want to be unkind," says Winnie, "but it's true. It's her intention to rot."

Mari prays that Fran can't overhear Winnie. There is no

knowing, Mari thinks, what Fran feels for the old lady or for Gorkey, who took her in, no knowing if she feels grateful or beholden, but one thing you can count on, Mari thinks, still playing with the potato's eye, she likely doesn't approve of customers discussing the smell of old Mrs. Gorkey.

"Shhhh." Mari can't help herself. "Shhh," she says again, tipping her head in the direction of Fran. Winnie looks perplexed. She lifts her head, her eyes stopping momentarily on the boys outside the store windows, young men snapping their fingers in a slow hip-gliding rhythm. Mari watches Winnie's eyes as they shift to Fran, who is perched on her three-legged stool. Winnie's eyes move back to Mari. Then, with a toss of her head toward the back of the store, she invites Mari to the rear, where Fran can't overhear.

Winnie turns on her toe. Mari follows.

"You know, I just figured it out." Winnie looks surprised at herself. Looks excited.

"What? Figured what out?"

"Well," says Winnie, "just walking back here, I recalled a recent diet article. And *boof!* Like a light bulb I figured out why she's getting . . ." Winnie pauses. Then says, "Okay, I'll say it. I hate to be unkind. I never want to be unkind. But there's no denying it. So I'll say it. Fatter. She's getting fatter every day. And I know why." She lifts a can of Comet, looks at herself in the top of the can's reflection.

"Who's fatter?"

Winnie puts down the Comet and looks at Mari with exasperation. She doesn't want to say, Mari knows. Winnie expects her to know. She wants a conversation in which no one is named.

Winnie flips the top of her head to the front of the store.

Fran, thinks Mari. Whose bottom spreads like bread dough over the lip of the three-legged stool. Fran with her immense cottage-cheese arms.

"Oh," says Mari.

"Listen: 'Dieters who are pushed onto the wagon usually fall off. Don't go on a diet for anyone except yourself.' Now here. Here's the cruncher: 'Count on conversation, not calories, to provide a feeling of well-being at mealtimes!'" Winnie tap taps her fingertips against the Comet tin.

"You have that memorized too?"

"That's not the point. The point is Fran. Who's she got to talk to?"

Mari shrugs. She hasn't spent much time contemplating Fran's mealtime company.

"You tell me who she's going to converse with instead of consuming calories. It's no wonder. Who does she talk to? Gorkey? He doesn't talk."

"Oh."

"Well, think about it. Have you ever had so much as a word with Gorkey? What has the man ever said to you?"

"He's shy."

"Which is all very well unless you're talking about mealtime chats. Naturally he's nice. Must have a great heart to have taken her in. But he's lacking on the conversation front."

"Mmmmm. I guess so."

"Well, it just makes you sad to think about. So lonely for her. All those empty, empty hours with nothing to do but eat. And the old lady. Word has it she talks, but she won't leave her deathbed. Would you want to have your evening meal at the foot of someone's deathbed? Not on your life. So she eats alone. Up there in her little empty room. Sits on the single chair by the window and eats and eats and eats." Winnie checks her mascara with the Comet tin. She pulls at a lower lash.

Mari wonders if she ought to pick up a Comet tin too and check the outline of her brow. Instead she snaps open her handbag and pulls out her du Mauriers.

"Now, I bet you're going to suggest Cora as company."

Mari squints against the smoke as she lights her cigarette. "I was," she says. She blows smoke from the side of her mouth. "She's a fine daughter."

"When she's around."

"Well?" As Winnie puts down the tin of Comet and opens her purse, Mari recognizes how Winnie runs a conversation. She holds out bits of sugar. Gives a sampling and waits to be asked for more. "Where's she been?"

"Up at the graveyard of course."

"And?"

"Well, nothing. She eats up there. Up Little Cypress in the graveyard. She's not here to give her mother company." Winnie pulls out her lipstick, winds the color up, then lifts her Comet.

Mari takes a drag of her cigarette. She knows Winnie is waiting for her to ask why the girl would be up there. Mari lifts her chin to the ceiling, blows a smoke ring and says, "Now, why, Winnie, would she be eating her lunch in the graveyard?"

Winnie wiggles her lips back and forth to even out the color. Then she polishes the top of the Comet can with her finger. "Fran sends her."

"That's a strange thing to do."

"Not if you know firsthand the trouble that can come from hanging out with nasty boys at the storefront."

"Oh."

"She's got to keep her daughter safe. Fran can't have history repeating itself. She has to keep her in the graveyard."

Winnie points to the teens outside.

Mari watches them sway to a low-down music which moves through their changing bodies. She believes she can hear the Elvis songs they sing out loud into the sky: "Love me tender, love me . . ."

"See that? Now wouldn't you call that moving in a baby-making sort of way?"

"I don't know that I'd call it that exactly. They're just young boys singing."

"Fran can't risk history repeating itself," says Winnie again.

Mari taps ash onto the hardwood floor, rubs it in with a sandaled toe. She shrugs.

"Fran watches these teens every single day." Winnie puts her tube of lipstick back into her purse and snaps it shut. "Those teenage boys gather up girls with their eyes. If I've said it once, I've said it a million times: If I let them, they would eat the pearls from my neck. And I know that Fran, watching those pimply boys with their bulging adam's apples, is considering the boy who fathered Cora." Winnie takes a deep breath, whispers into Mari's face, "They've got those Elvis songs in their mouths and those things in their pants."

"Winnie!" Mari drops her cigarette, grinds it out on the floor.

"Well, it's true. And if anyone knows about that, it's Fran. So she has to send Cora up to the graveyard." Winnie puts the Comet tin back on the shelf. "If Fran had behaved one iota as she was supposed to, she would never have gotten pregnant." And Winnie picks up her *Woman's Home Companion.*

Mari decides then that she'd much rather be deadheading her petunias. She knows, as Winnie lifts her face to yet another article, that nothing compares to the joy of being in her garden, despite Davy Crockett.

"Y'know," says Winnie, "maybe if Fran's hometown had had Dr. Johnson, Fran would have kept her legs crossed. I think the good doctor's articles keep our town on the right track."

"I get tired of them. Really tired." Mari lifts Winnie's tin of Comet and puts it in her shopping cart. She doesn't care, suddenly, what Winnie, with her little white teeth and matching pearls, thinks.

"Just look at his son. Now there's an example—"

"I feel sorry for him," says Mari. And she pushes her cart past Winnie saying, "My garden's waiting. So is Elwood."

"Say hello to the little fella for me."

Mari suddenly stops and snaps open her handbag. Without knowing why, she lifts out the photograph of Elwood taken at the baseball game with Howard. Before handing it over to Winnie, Mari looks at the happy figures caught in black and white, sees Elwood in a baseball cap, his mouth open as he jumps into the air. His father beside him, both of them wild with joy, a bag of popcorn in Elwood's hand.

Mari, without a word to Winnie, extends the photograph. Surrounded by Chore Boys and dishwashing liquid, Mari watches Winnie's nutmeg-mottled hands reach out for her photo of Elwood. Her fingers move across the surface of Elwood and his father.

The strawberry hair on the back of Winnie's hands lifts. Mari looks up, watches a disturbance like wind gusting against the blue sky of Winnie's eyes. "What?" says Mari in a low voice. "What is it?"

Winnie's lips form a white line.

"Please," says Mari.

"Who did this to him? Who wrapped him up?"

"He's smiling. Isn't he smiling?"

Winnie looks at Mari and says, "No."

"Well, what then? What?"

Winnie lifts Mari's hand, brings Mari's finger to the photograph and runs it over Elwood. Once, twice and again until Mari begins slowly to feel what her eyes cannot see. She feels his wrapped body, his mummy-tight torso.

Mari realizes her boy is not smiling. He is searching for air and his arms, up and out, are grasping, his fingers clawing for air.

"I'd be up all night talking to Howard about this if I were you," says Winnie.

Mari snaps the photo back in her handbag. She looks at Winnie, but Winnie, who's picked up her *Woman's Home Companion* again, has her eyes firmly on the words in her magazine.

"Winnie," says Mari, "I just want to thank you."

"Listen to this," says Winnie. "'Not long ago, the current Mrs. America was asked by a photographer to lift her skirts so that he could get a picture of her legs. She declined gently but firmly. 'I don't pose for cheesecake,' she said. 'I bake it!'

"'Her remark pointed to one of the most interesting phenomena of our time—the evolution of a top national contest, stressing the ideal in woman, from a bathing-beauty show into a serious home economics tournament, all in eighteen brief years. The judges of Mrs. America today are no longer looking for a woman of perfect physical proportions, but rather an outstanding wife, cook, homemaker and general pillar of the community. In short, the bikini has been replaced by the apron; the swimming pool by the kitchen range.'"

Winnie lifts her face from her *Woman's Home Companion*, "There you go," she says.

~

Mari, still squatting over her lily, becomes aware of her aching knees. She can't stay on the ground protecting her lily from the wind forever. And the wind doesn't seem to be dying. So what, she wonders, can she do with her lily? Cardboard. She will build a cardboard circle of protection. But she'll have to get Elwood/Davy to cradle her lily while she makes it.

"Elwood," she calls to the gun sounds behind the poplar. "Elwood!"

Nothing.

"Davy. Davy Crockett."

And out from behind the tree he runs. "Yes'm. What can I do for you today, little woman?"

"Just come here. Put your hands here. Like this. And don't move. No matter what, don't take your hands away."

Mari takes his small hands and curves them around her lily. "Now stay!" she says and runs to the garage to find cardboard.

"But I've got things to do. There's been an attack up the hill."

"In a minute. You can go in just a minute."

# Elwood

ELWOOD DOES NOT WANT to stay bent over a stupid lily. Not at all. He glances over his shoulder, watches his mother enter the garage. Like Davy, he could just get on with what he ought to be getting on with. *You know me,* Davy says to his wife, the two of them in front of the fire, *when I'm sure I'm right, I go ahead.* The wild frontier calls. Elwood is right to abandon his mother's lily.

Elwood looks down at the lily one more time. The plant is no longer a lily but two baby alligators deep in the grass. *Baby gators,* says Davy's sidekick Russel, as they come upon them in the back woods. Davy and Russel are on foot, sneaking through the bush, looking for warriors. *I'm more scared of snakes and gators,* says Russel, *than I am of injuns.*

Davy smiles his slow smile, looks down at the alligators. *Kinda cute, ain't they?*

That's how baby gators or a lily can be, when you're wearing your coonskin, thinks Elwood. *Kinda cute, ain't they?* Elwood thinks about his mother asking him to protect her lily. He smiles a slow smile. "I'm plumb flutterated with that honor," he says aloud to the lily.

But if a lily's kinda cute when you're wearing a coonskin, what is it when you're wearing a baseball cap? A baseball cap is way different. With a baseball cap you don't say things like *Reckon I gotta learn you how.* Never. What you says is *Catch it, you idiot!*

~

"Steeeerike one. . . ."

"Ha!" the father blasts. Popcorn falls out of his mouth, lands on his lap. He hits the son's back. "One down, two to go. He'll strike out for sure."

The son hits the father's back. "Yup," he says. "Sure will."

They smile at each other. Buddies. As long as he's wearing the baseball cap, thinks the son. Then they are buddies and he isn't in his room or being shaken, the colors in his head like a kaleidoscope spinning too fast.

"Let me tell you right now, young man, you won't be wearing that goofy coonskin to the game," his father had said.

"I like it."

"I know you like it. But it's not what you wear to baseball games."

"Why not?"

"Because. Don't argue."

"I'm not. But why not?"

"At baseball games you wear a baseball cap. When you go to church, you wear nice clothes. Your mother wears a hat and nice gloves to church. She doesn't wear her gardening gloves to church any more than you wear that goofy hat to the game."

"Why not?"

"For god's sake, Elwood! If your mother wore gardening gloves to church people would figure she was either a commie or she had some kind of mental illness, which she likely would have if she wore her gardening gloves to church. Understand?"

"Not really."

"Here it is for you, simple: If you want to get on in the world, look at what others are doing or wearing and do or wear it."

"But I—"

"You haven't heard a damn word I've said. Not one. At baseball games you wear baseball caps, and it's just as simple as the sky is blue."

Elwood dips his face to the darkness of his hands, must refrain from saying, "Grey, the sky is grey." He must not say he has worked hard to see the grey, that the last time his father shook him by the shoulders, colors exploded behind his eyes, crimson blossoms flew like birds to the clouds. Cobalt rained on the grass. All upside down his stomach dizzy, his ears hurting with the sound of shattering colors.

The TV fixed him. He watched until he learned the color grey. Knew how to see the sky and the grass as grey. He learned words people like to hear. He learned how to wave, how to make his father smile. On the TV the skies are grey and all is well.

So Elwood, with his face in his palms, does not argue with his father, does not tell him he's wrong about the blue sky. Instead he lets his father put the baseball cap on his head. Now he is not a commie or a mental illness.

"Steeeerikkke two!"

"Ha!" Elwood laughs. Popcorn falls out of his mouth. One unpopped kernel rolls from his lap onto the father's, where it lodges in the crease in his pants between groin and thigh. *Thwack!*

The father jumps to his feet, "Catch it! Catch it, you idiot!"

Then he turns to look at Elwood. *Stand up, stand up stand up* his eyes say, and Elwood sees that everyone else is standing, which means he must stand and shout, "Catch it, you idiot!"

*Boof!* The flash of a camera.

~

His mother walks toward him through the wind with a piece of cardboard and some tape. "Thanks, sweetie," she says.

Elwood closes his eyes to the lemon sound of her voice.

Grey, he whispers to his eyelids. Black and white. For some reason he continues to see color in his mother's words. "Don't call me sweetie, damn it! Davy. Call me Davy or nothing, lady."

"Davy," she says as she hunkers beside him in the wind with her cardboard. "You go on up the hill," she says, her voice now dark. "Sandwiches are made. So's the lemonade. Take them. And don't let me hear you speak like that again."

# *Winnie*

WINNIE SORTS HER LAUNDRY, carefully separating the whites into five loads. One for Frank's shirts. Another for her blouses, bras and panties. A third for the girls' white knee socks and blouses. Sheets, white sheets from the beds she changes weekly, make up the fourth. Everything else is dark and goes into one pile.

There is no color on Winnie's laundry room floor. She hasn't seen color in ages, so she doesn't buy it.

Except lipstick. Winnie buys all shades of lipstick. Learns stylish lipstick colors from the magazine ads and buys by name.

In the laundry room sink Winnie has a galvanized pail in which she bleaches the girls' white socks. She'll add these to the load with their blouses later. Winnie bends to the laundry, telling herself, "'There is no finer career than homemaking.'" She's read this recently in an article in *Woman's Home Companion.* "Women who turn to other professions for glamor don't know what glamor really is." This, thinks Winnie, lifting one of Frank's shirts and placing it gingerly in the pile, spoken by someone who should know, Mrs. America herself.

Winnie pauses, stands straight, rubs the small of her back with the flats of her palms and thinks how well those sleeping pills work. Amazing man, that Dr. Johnson. To have just the right thing. Winnie looks out the small basement window up to the poplars with their branches swaying in the wind, the shiny undersides of leaves flashing in the morning light, and recalls her visit with Dr. Johnson.

~

"I'm not sleeping." She sits in the chair opposite him. Sits with her hands tucked into the folds of her navy skirt. She will not take chances with his seeing her hands, will not give him the opportunity to see her freckles, which have begun to stir beneath her skin.

"Not at all?"

"No, I'm up all night." Which isn't quite true. She is sleeping some of the time. But she resists sleep.

Wake and sleep dance a tango while Winnie sits in the hard chair at the dining room table, telling Frank to leave her be. "I'll be there in just a minute. You go on. I want to finish my magazine." And Winnie, alone in the night, sets to memorizing. Anything to resist sleep. For if sleep wins, Winnie must face her mother, Bride, who moves back into Winnie's body while she sleeps. Bride wears a muted scarlet hobo quilt over her shoulders.

In these dreams her mother has her arms wrapped around a huge bundle of colorful grasses, seeds and blossoms. Her arms are bare. Delicate sinews of muscle, thin vertical lines, run up her arms. Her thin arms do not touch. Her fingers, long and unfurling, become the grass.

The long grass sweeps from grey to emerald and into an explosion of blossoms. Tansy, goldenrod, daisybain, clover, tiger lily, northern bedstraw, bergamot. Names Winnie has banned from her thoughts.

"Are you ready yet?" asks Bride, pulling at the hobo quilt, releasing the heavy scent of creosote. "Surely you've had enough of *Woman's Home Companion*."

In these dreams Winnie moves toward her mother, arms outstretched, but hesitates. With every dream the distance between them closes. When Winnie wakes she is worried and ashamed. She spends extra time brushing her girls' hair, puts a roast in the oven even though it's not Sunday. Joins another committee.

Winnie will stay awake all night, if that's what it takes. She will sit up hour after hour telling Frank, who pleads with her to enter his arms, that she's not tired. "I napped this afternoon," she tells him. "While the girls played Barbies I fell asleep just like that in the backyard. It was so warm."

But she tells the doctor she is not sleeping. Not at all.

"Mmmmm," he says. "Too young, aren't you, for the change of life. Sleeplessness can accompany such a time. No, it's not that." He looks straight at her and rubs his chin with his hand.

"I admire you, Winnie. Frankly, it's women like you who make me realize my efforts in this community are worthwhile. But sometimes there is a cost to being so involved."

"Like not sleeping?"

"Exactly. You get too wound up thinking of this and that. You're on the PTA, aren't you? And the Red Cross. A member of your church. A mother of two small children, not to mention Frank's wife. It's a lot, isn't it?"

Winnie nods.

"Perhaps something should give way."

Winnie, who wants sleeping pills, says, "I couldn't give up the PTA."

"No, no. That's an important one."

"The Red Cross?"

"No. I shouldn't think so. They need devoted ladies like you."

"Obviously I can't give up the church or my children. It's simply a busy time, doctor. If I can do it, others will believe they can too."

"Of course," says the Doctor swiveling his chair back and forth.

"But without sleep I can't function. I can't do it all."

The doctor lifts his arm, begins to play with the soft fold of skin under his chin.

Winnie clears her throat, opens her handbag and slips her gloves onto her hands as though she intends to leave. Then slowly she brings her hand to the pearls on her neck and twirls them, one at a time. "'Our ideal married woman,'" Winnie reminds the Doctor, "'is gifted with personality and charm as well as the ability to bake, sew, shop, plan menus, iron a shirt, work for the PTA and her church and keep her husband happy at the same time.'"

"Yes," says the doctor, "of course."

"I need my sleep."

The doctor rises from his chair. "I think of us as a team, Winnie. We have the same ideas about things. We both want to set high standards for our community."

"Exactly," says Winnie.

"You set an example, Winnie, of what a lady can accomplish when she wants to." The Doctor turns and opens a cupboard. "I'll write you a prescription, but you can start with these. Two before bed."

"Thank-you," says Winnie, curling her fingers around the white bottle.

"I like to see ladies like you taking responsibility for their health."

Winnie places the capsules in her handbag and snaps it shut. Then, as though Bride has taken control of her body, she says, "I never once said that women should pass a cooking test before getting their marriage license. You misquoted me in your newspaper article."

"What are you talking about?"

Winnie clamps her mouth shut. She mustn't let Bride speak again.

"You certainly are all wound up, aren't you? Tight as a drum. The pills will help."

Winnie, in her basement, closes her eyes to the wind and the way it makes the grass beckon. Sleep, she thinks. Ah, sleep. A sweet thing with these tiny white pills. There's no sinking slowly into asleep, she thinks, pushing the ivory sheets into her new electric washing machine. One moment she's awake, the next she's asleep.

Then all at once it's morning. The walls are white and it's morning and the night is behind her. Frank rolls toward the white wall, rolls over to turn off the alarm, and there is no evidence that time has passed except the walls are white rather than dark as they were before she shut her eyes.

Another advantage, thinks Winnie, pushing at a pair of Frank's underwear with the toe of her polished shoe, is she doesn't need to go buying lipstick in her mind while Frank moves inside her. No. She simply closes her eyes.

So Bride, for the time being, is held at bay. Winnie's secret is safe in the gauzy confines of sleeping pills.

## A Fine Daughter

~

Winnie's secret begins with Bride and the quilts. Quilts sewn by mothers and sisters, stitched carefully by women talking together, teasing one another. Reds and greens, purple and golden yellow sewn into patterns.

Then came the hard time. The dark time, when the prairies dried up. The dark soil lifted into the flat prairie sky and the sun burned the earth. Families were forced to move. They packed what could fit on a wagon and left. Sons and daughters often went toward the tracks, holding a quilt and perhaps a photograph, a skein of hair, a penny whistle or harmonica. By day they rode the freight trains and looked for work. At night they wrapped themselves in quilts beside the track or in boxcars.

Many ended up at one time or another, riding the CNR to Mirror, Winnie's home town. There, not too far from the tracks, the earth leaked gas. The hobos knew it. Lit a match, held it to the earth and a fire was lit. The hobos were drawn to Mirror by the gas leaks, but they stayed for the soup that Bride, Winnie's mother, made for them.

As a young girl of ten, Winnie visits the hobo jungle with Bride. Together, in the evenings, they bring soup made from plants scrounged from the earth to the homesick down by the tracks. They stop on the lip of the hill, see distant fires dotting the valley. Around the fires hobos huddle in quilts muted and grey with creosote. Someone plays a harmonica, the low sad tune lifting across the dark of the night.

Bride wears big skirts. Keeps her pipe burning in her skirt pocket while she walks among the hobos. She holds Winnie's hand, carries a big pot of soup against her hip like a baby. Pipe smoke and creosote.

Bride nods at most, talks to some. With her soup still steaming on her hip, she'll pause to listen to stories about stacking wood for a week in a lumber mill just outside of Penticton or of picking potatoes the size of thumbnails near Bentley. But every now and then Bride lowers her soup to the ground and, lifting her skirts, squats beside the curled posture of a man. She touches his back and says, "You're low, son. How long have you been away?"

Bride has told Winnie about hobo homesickness. "Some," she says, "are natural-born drifters, but most have the home at the center of their hearts. Oh, you'll hear them laugh now and then, Winnie, but what these people want more than anything is to be home." Sending the hobos home is Bride's specialty. She gives them soup made from plants scrounged from the earth and let's it ferry them home.

"Take small amounts of tansy," Bride has told Winnie. "Look for the startling yellow. It's poisonous but, in small amounts, it's powerful. And clary sage. Best that it's clary, good for dreams and inspiring the imagination. You'll see the silver green in the mornings. Add some purple. Daisybain and a snippet of hyssop. The white of cow parsnip."

As a thank-you, the hobos give Bride what they have. She refuses gifts, but can't give back what she finds on her porch steps first thing in the morning. So Bride and Winnie sometimes wake to find quilts folded up and smelling of creosote. Sometimes drifters have left a woman's braid or a lace doily. A harmonica. Bride's cupboards become heavy with the weight of gifts and the smell of the railway tracks.

But it is not the sick heavy smell of creosote which begins Winnie's rejection of her mother. It's the piano. It confirms in people's minds what's already suspected about Bride.

People Winnie does not know stand in their kitchen, saying to Bride, "Keep it for us until we get back. Things will get better." The piano is delivered on a big wagon drawn by two horses. The piano sits up there with its teeth smiling away for all the world to see. A piano is one thing. The town understands pianos, but this is a player piano. Pump with your feet and the keys move.

Winnie's home is already out of bounds for most children Winnie's age. But that doesn't keep them from peering in the windows at night, when Bride and Winnie can't see them. They see Bride's unmoving hands and the piano's keys going up and down and hear music filling the air. Soon the story spreads among the town's children that Winnie's mother is a witch. They taunt Winnie, tell her she stinks like a train.

So Winnie quits dressing up in the quilts the hobos leave behind. She pretends Bride isn't her mother.

They sit one night on the front porch. The northern lights are green, colors shifting and dancing like piano keys. Bride hums low in her throat with the same sad resonance of a harmonica. Then she stops and into this silence Bride says, "Harriet lives in Blackfalds. My sister. You can go there. Live with her."

Winnie stands and nods. Right then she can feel Bride leave, feels her body empty. She looks up and the northern lights flood grey. Fine by me, thinks Winnie. If that's the price, I can do without color.

~

Winnie carries a white plastic basketful of damp blouses up from the basement. She steps into the wind, pauses on the back stoop with the basket on her hip, brings her free hand to her hair to hold it back from her face. What a strange day. So hot despite the wind. So bright, thinks Winnie, looking past the sheets already on the line and up toward Little Cypress Hill. There she sees Cora's young figure, the wind lifting her long hair behind her like wings.

The poor child, thinks Winnie, up there all alone. Like Rapunzel in her tower. Winnie steps from her back porch, moves across the lawn with the wind blowing her skirt behind her. She holds it down with the flat of her hand, thinking how Fran is just like the witch in Rapunzel. Winnie sets her laundry basket on the ground.

Damn it, she thinks and closes her eyes to sees Bride with her hand stretched toward her. Fingertips of grass, fireweed burning in her palms. Winnie thinks again of Cora so like Rapunzel in the tower. She considers how, despite her isolation, Rapunzel had a visitor. Still managed, though she was hidden away by the witch, to conceive. Oh yes, thinks Winnie, Rapunzel had a baby.

Winnie knows she can't let herself think such thoughts. She needs her *Woman's Home Companion*. "What is your family really like?" a recent article asked. "What are their goals? Their needs? Their interests?" When the witch discovered Rapunzel's suitor, thinks Winnie, trying to recall what she's supposed to know about her family, the witch flung him from the window and he was blinded on a rosebush. Rapunzel gave birth and the father of her baby wandered blind until he found her.

Winnie stills her hands, thinks how Rapunzel cried when she saw the man. And it was one of her tears rolling from her cheek to his eyes, which restored his sight.

Winnie shakes her head. She'll never get the laundry done if she keeps wasting time. Still, as Winnie lifts her hand to the line, as she anchors part of the blouse to the wire with a wooden peg, she thinks of sorrow. What, she wonders, does Rapunzel say of women's sorrow?

Winnie lifts the other half of the blouse to the line, secures it with a pin and bends again to her basket. "Save your back by taking a strong position for activities such as ironing or washing clothes," she tells herself. "Bend forward from the hips, keeping back and shoulders in a straight line from hips to top of head." Winnie straightens her back, tries to remember the photo of the woman in her magazine. She wore a black leotard to do her housework so the women who bought the magazine could see her straight spine. "If you prefer to sit down when you do your ironing, we suggest you follow the directions for using a sewing machine."

Winnie pulls another white blouse from her basket, shakes it, thinking as it snaps and flickers across her face, that she ought to hurry. Ought to get this work done. It must be almost half past eight. But there's something in this wind, she thinks, gathering the blouse into her arms and holding it as she looks to the sky.

Winnie lifts the blouse to her face, smells the cool dampness. The wind presses it against her eyes and for a moment she is blinded. Although she has washed this blouse, run it through her new washer with Tide, she believes she can smell Fran. Embedded in the cloth is Fran's Lily-of-the-Valley talcum powder and her fat-lady sweat.

Yes, it is Fran, Winnie thinks, Fran's scent. Fran, opening the door for her as she left Gorkey's, grazing her shoulder, so Winnie felt the dampness of her hot body.

~

The warmth of Fran's body blushes through the white shoulder of Winnie's blouse. "She's done it. Fran's done it," thinks

Winnie, lifting her head as she passes the singing boys and the girls with their Hula-Hoops circling their widening hips. Not sex, but birth. Winnie shifts the brown paper bag on her hip and considers Fran who, the whole town knows, birthed Cora without ether. Birthed her without twilight sleep. Fran, seventeen and with only a nurse to assist her, birthed Cora without so much as an Aspirin.

The warmth of Fran's body reminds her of flesh and thighs, bawdy and ample. Which, as she steps onto the curb and pauses, looking for traffic, reminds her of Fran's pain.

Thank god for ether, thinks Winnie, crossing the street, nodding a thank-you to Howard, who waits in his car for her to cross. How civilized to go to the hospital with her little overnight bag packed and her largeness well covered with a bulky overcoat. How nice to put down her bag and remove her clothes in privacy, put on the clean hospital gown and wait for the ether. Of course, there was some pain, some discomfort. But before pain could take hold of her body she was long gone. Awake once the baby was nice and clean.

It doesn't bear thinking about, Fran's ordeal. Really, Winnie thinks, shouldering the door of her husband's barbershop, if Dr. Johnson were capable of sin, it was letting that poor child have a baby without so much as twilight sleep.

Frank's not in, which is good. Winnie puts her bag of groceries on the counter and leaves. He'll bring them home later.

Back on Main Street Winnie steps, chest thrust forward. Her thought about Dr. Johnson is unfair. He really tried to be there on time. But, as Stella later explained to anyone interested in knowing, her husband simply couldn't get there. "Those girls," he'd told her and she repeated, "tend to give birth quickly."

Which, of course, confirmed what everyone already believed about Fran. She was, Winnie thinks, loose.

Still, Winnie wonders, pausing now to lift the heel of her right foot and to straighten her hose, what was it like to labor, to give birth? And although she would like to deny it, Winnie knows that she, like most of the women in town, is awed by Fran, who birthed her baby and knew it.

Winnie is halfway up Main when she realizes she left her *Woman's Home Companion* with the groceries. "For heaven's sake," she mutters, turning on her heel. Winnie marches back to the barbershop and—thank goodness!—Frank's still not in.

~

The wind lifts Winnie's hair. She brings one hand to her forehead, pushing her hair back, and sets to pinning her Fran-scented blouse to the line. Why is she daydreaming today? What is making her drift and meander like this? Winnie pulls her shoulders back. She prefers clear thinking, black-and-white thinking. It's safe.

"What is your family really like? What are their goals? Their needs?" Room to play for the girls. More Barbie dresses. More little plastic Barbie shoes. Apart from that, her girls need nothing. Their clothes are clean. They are well fed. She reads Beatrix Potter to them every single night.

Frank must be happy. Three clean shirts a day if he wants. Clean socks. A wife who wears pearls and knows how to keep her nails long and buffed despite housework. Who has a twenty-eight–inch waist but a healthy thirty-eight–inch bust. Not bad, thinks Winnie, after two children.

So why, wonders Winnie, bending again to her basket, had he

reached for her in the kitchen last week saying with such intensity as his hand wrapped round her wrist, "Forget the washing and the cooking and your damn magazines."

Oh Frank, she thinks, don't you know what my magazines do for you? They give you a wife. A good wife.

"Please," he says, pulling her to his hips, "put it down. Put it all down and come to bed." Frank in the darkening kitchen puts his arms around Winnie, flattens his palms against her thighs, pulls her hips toward his body, puts his lips against her forehead. "Oh Winnie," he whispers to her temple. "Where are you?" He places his palms on either side of her head, squeezes until she is afraid her head will open and who knows what will come flying out.

"For god's sake, Frank! Stop it!"

He drops his hands. "Sorry."

Winnie steps back, saying, as she brings her hands to rub where his have pressed, "I don't know what's gotten into you lately. I really don't." She backs farther from him until her back presses against the counter. "I do all I can to keep you happy, and it never seems to be enough."

Frank opens his mouth as if to speak but says nothing.

"The first Mrs. America winner," thinks Winnie, "Mrs. Margaret Chamberlain, a model, was selected on beauty alone. Nobody knew, or cared, whether she could fry an egg or wash out a pair of socks. As things turned out, Mrs. Chamberlain could do both these things exceedingly well. Perhaps that is why she is still happily married to the same husband."

Winnie brings her hand to Frank's chin. "I don't think you have a thing to complain about," she says.

Winnie pushes her hair back, reaches into her apron pocket

for another clothespin. "What is your family really like? What are their goals? Their needs? Their interests? If you know, with certainty"—Winnie pulls another blouse from the basket and reaches again for the line—"you will have a successful living room."

Winnie walks around to the clothesline, where her first load of sheets are hung. She brings each to her face, breathes a scent more sweet than a spring morning breeze, a scent sweet as the first lick of vanilla ice cream on a blistering day. What, wonders Winnie, turning from her sheets, lifting her hand to the wind, is happening?

She looks up the hill again and sees Cora still at the top. Knows that Cora, like Rapunzel, will become pregnant. She tells herself to stop thinking, to go back to her magazine and sleeping pills. But she can't. Suddenly Winnie wants the wind to carry her away. Just for now, she tells herself, she'll leave the laundry. She lies down on the cool grass. Silly, thinks Winnie, but it feels so good.

# Frank

FRANK, Winnie's husband, should be at work. He is supposed to be cutting hair. But he scurried through the wind to his shop, put a note within the doorframe and pressed home. He hopes people won't ask too many questions. But there's something in the wind which made him want to stay home this morning. Just like that. Stay home.

So he's drinking coffee at their breakfast table and hoping he won't feel guilty. Winnie will give him an earful. But until she discovers him in their kitchen, he'll just drink coffee and take pleasure in watching her hang laundry in the wind. But Winnie stops. Frank leans toward the window to make certain he's seeing correctly. Winnie is lying down on the lawn just a few feet from the window. This is something he's never seen before. Winnie outside flat on her back in her house dress. Legs wide, arms abandoned to the sky.

But of course, Frank tells himself as he questions whether he ought to be concerned, he's never in all his years with Winnie watched her hang laundry. She does laundry Saturday mornings. He cuts hair. Frank can't imagine Winnie stretched out like this every Saturday, but who's to know? There's very little he really knows about his wife.

## A Fine Daughter

Frank takes a gulp of his coffee, then another. Nothing beats coffee in the morning. He has this week's paper in front of him, sitting unread on Winnie's little white tablecloth, which looks to him like an oversized doily, though he'd never say so. The paper's there, ready to be read, but he can't. He's too excited just sitting here drinking coffee without having to sharpen the razor blades with his leather strop or wash the windows. No red and white barber pole to polish this morning. No. Just this coffee in the sun with his wife stretched out on the lawn. She still doesn't know he's home.

He moves to the stove, lifts the pot from the burner and rinses out what's left of the coffee. He'll make another pot. And another again if he feels like it. He'll drink it all this morning, and maybe, he thinks, he'll even march right out there with a cup for Winnie. He'll just step right out there into the wind and hand her a cup saying, *Here you are, Winnie, my sweet, a cup of coffee to brighten your day.*

Frank lifts the spoon of coffee grounds to his nose, sniffs so deeply he has to wipe grounds from his face. But so what. Of course Winnie would say, *Now, you know I don't drink coffee while I work.* Or, *It's not time. Coffee's at ten.* Or more likely, thinks Frank, pouring water into the bottom of the pot, Winnie would take her white pearls in hand, and say, *Why Frank! What are you doing home? You can't—*

*I decided not to work today.*

*You what?*

*I left a note. Here. Your coffee.*

*You can't. My good heavens, Frank. You have a responsibility.*

Frank pours sugar into his waiting cup. What fun. He can hear the girls in the next room. Their laughter lifts over the sound of the TV. He moves back to his newspaper, drops his head to read. But he can't. It's too wonderful sitting in the sun, just sitting here. Frank looks out the window to Winnie.

Amazing, given all the clean shirts, all the white socks and folded hankies, that he's never seen her do laundry. Not that she's doing much at the moment. Frank, looking at Winnie stretched out on the lawn, thinks how strange that he should love his wife from afar. Such lovely long arms, he thinks, her freckles racing along them, her hair wild as foxtail in the wind. His Winnie. He wants in a desperate way to go to her, to lift her pearls from her, to dip his head into the pools of scent lingering in the nape of her neck.

Frank drops his head to his paper. He wonders quite suddenly, as the image of Winnie on the porch fades, if this is what life in the middle years comes to. That he should wonder time and again if he had proposed to one Winnie and married another.

Frank takes another gulp of his coffee, looks again at Winnie lying on the lawn. He watches her chest rise and fall, notes the lush blue of the veins on the inside of her wrists and something, perhaps the angle of her legs, convinces Frank that the Winnie he proposed to is the woman outside the window.

"Marry me, Winnie. Please, won't you, please?"

Frank at twenty wants to touch her red hair. Wants that hair next to his on a pillow. Frank can't keep his eyes still as he speaks. "I'll take you to my town—Little Cypress—it's a nice place, Winnie, with a hill for picnicking and a fire station." Frank wants to kiss each freckle on her long arms, wants to feel her thighs beneath his.

"I need to think about it. I'm keen to stay on in Calgary."

"But Winnie, I'm all set to start up, you know. I've got my shop. Got my papers and ready-made clientele. Even got my shirts." Frank winks at Winnie; she'd helped him pick them out, her hands freckled as starling's eggs, thrusting one, then another to his arms to try on.

~

Winnie is nineteen and has landed her first job at Eaton's selling hot dogs. Frank buys a hot dog from her. "Where's Men's Wear?"

Winnie begins to point, then says, "I'll take you. I intend to advance to Woman's Wear. This'll be a start."

"I need shirts for starting out as a barber."

Winnie tells her co-worker that she's doing a stint in Men's Wear, and says to Frank, "Follow me, please."

Frank, whose intention is only to buy shirts, is moved by Winnie's hands. Winnie, carrying armloads of checkered olive green and pumpkin-colored shirts, makes Frank sweat.

He's too polite to tell her he can't possibly try them all on.

"Here," she says, dropping one more shirt into his open arms, "this one's pink. It's the look this fall." Winnie drops another shirt and another into his arm. Her words are crisp as the collars. "Stylish," she says of one. "Enviable. Tasteful. Smart." But its her hands he continues to watch.

Finally he touches her hand as though to stop the procession of shirts. He holds her hand, but can't say the words. He looks closely at the white petals of her fingers. Her nails are bitten to the quick.

"You," he says, smiling at her, "have nice hands."

~

"I'm not so sure about marrying you, Frank," says Winnie much later. "I don't want to live in a small town. I want the city. I want face cream and the newest fashions—"

Frank quickly grabs her hand, brings her thumbnail to his mouth. Bites into the nail. Tastes sweet clover and earthy afternoons. "Come, Winnie."

Winnie pulls her hand from his mouth. Rolls on the grass away from him. With a surprising quickness she nips the stems of yarrow, begins to braid them together.

Frank sits up, leans toward a yarrow stem, takes it between thumb and forefinger, tries to nip it but can't. "How'd you do that?"

She shrugs. "Look, I have plans. I've just left a small town. Why move to Little Cypress?"

He crawls along the grass to her, nudges her with the top of his head, sniffs at her neck and smells a lazy heat. "Oh God, Winnie. You've got to."

Winnie pushes at his nudging head with the palm of her hand. "Would you cut that out! Now listen, Frank. I mean this." Winnie sits up straight. "I *want* to marry a man from the city. You're not. I *want* to marry a well-connected man."

"Folk in Little Cypress think highly of me, Winnie."

"Shhhh. I was saying, I *want* to marry a man who will allow me to have my hair done two times a week."

Frank lifts his hands to her hair and says, "You bet."

"I *want* two children, and I have a weakness for lipstick, magazines and coffee." Winnie pulls her skirt over her knees.

Frank, lost in the aroma of sweet clover, its sultry yellow scent, reaches for her. Wraps his arms round her shoulders and says, "Sounds like you're shopping for fruit."

"I mean it, Frank. Every word. Are you prepared to go to church every Sunday?"

"Well, Winnie, look. If my going to church will make you happy, I'll go. But I never thought you were so religious."

"Religion has nothing to do with church. I plan on being an upstanding member of the community. Which means I'll go to church. Wash my windows on Tuesday. Plant geraniums in my windowboxes. Raise two happy children."

"I can live with that. But I've got to do it in Little Cypress."

Winnie sticks her finger into his chest, pushes him away. "I mean it," she says.

"So do I."

Winnie lifts the braided yarrow to his head and says, "Okay then." She even goes so far as to squeeze him. Right on the thigh.

~

Frank moves from the kitchen table to the window to see Winnie clearly. Stretched upon the lawn close to the window, Winnie is entirely relaxed, her eyes open. Frank wonders what she's watching. He looks closely at her eyes, sees movement reflected. Something up there is moving, he thinks. He pours a cup of coffee for Winnie and heads to the back door. He steps outside but Winnie's gone.

"Winnie!" Frank calls into the wind, wanting the lazy heat that lingers between Winnie's breasts. "Winnie," he shouts again, the wind filling his mouth with a taste of apples that makes his desire to see Winnie urgent. He leaves the coffee on the step and moves to the lawn, sniffing the turbulent air. Winnie must be behind the white sheets. He's certain. He pulls back the sheet to find Winnie's house dress billowing carelessly on the grass.

# The Good Doctor

DR. JOHNSON, in the back room of Gorkey's General, is thankful to be out of the exhausting wind. Letting his eyes adjust to the back room's dim light, he recalls the inquisitive housewives he passed on the street. Housewives who poked their heads out of doors, then, seeing the churning sky, ran down the front paths to get a better look. They all seemed to sniff the air, thought the doctor. Children ran up and down the streets as charged with energy as the sky. Men working in their yards abandoned their rakes and lawnmowers to watch the sky. The doctor, feeling his hair lift from his scalp, as though charged with electricity, called out, "A storm is coming," to the housewives, who simply ignored him. "Time to go home," he called to children, who merely laughed.

~

"The old lady's cough is worse," Gorkey had told him on the phone early this morning. Having established it wasn't an emergency, the doctor let himself sleep just a little longer and then penned a brief article for "What the Doctor Says" before braving the wind and the strange sky to listen to the old lady's lungs.

Her skin is a sheet pulled over her bones, white toffee which he can lift between his thumb and forefinger. Unexposed to sunlight or fresh air, Mrs. Gorkey's skin is transparent. He looks along her arm at the sapphire veins beneath the skin. Her bones are an elegant sweep of white, just discernible in the half-light. The doctor is aware of Gorkey, who's pacing behind him. Gorkey stops at the doctor's back.

"Like I said, she's coughing a lot. And she's tired. Very tired."

"I'll have to take a listen." The doctor drops his black bag at the foot of the bed. Gorkey begins pacing again.

Dr. Johnson pulls his stethoscope from the bag and can't resist checking himself in Mrs. Gorkey's mirror. The good doctor, he thinks. He lifts his chin. A soft pouch of skin is forming there, just loose skin, the kind that gathers with the years. The first sign of aging. Maybe he'll start wearing turtlenecks, the more relaxed look, the casual doctor. The doctor adjusts the stethoscope and smiles into the mirror. Still, not bad.

"I should have called earlier maybe, but I didn't want to wake you."

"No need to worry about that, Mr. Gorkey. My work is never done. I'm up with the sun." Dr. Johnson bends to Mrs. Gorkey, looks over his shoulder to Gorkey. "Would you please be still."

"Sorry."

"It's distracting."

"Sorry. I mean, well, I'm worried about Mother. But the store's not being watched either."

"Where's Fran? Where's your help?"

Gorkey shrugs. "She's probably gone to the train station. Morning train's in."

"I never heard it arrive with the wind making all that noise."

"Fran likes going to the station. Says it's always a surprise to see what's come down the tracks."

"You order your goods, don't you?"

"Of course."

"Then you know what's coming. There are no surprises."

Again, Gorkey shrugs. "In all her seventeen years here, she's never been late."

"The daughter then."

Gorkey shakes his head. "Cora's not here either."

"You're getting the runaround. You'd best get out front. I'll check your mother. I'll call if I need you."

"Fine. Yes. I'll go. But doctor, Fran's not unreliable."

Reliable, thinks the doctor as the door closes behind Gorkey, means here. She is not here. She is not reliable. That's what you get, thinks the doctor, turning again to the old lady, for hiring someone whose morals aren't up to standard.

The old lady hasn't coughed once since he's been here. If it weren't for the slight rising and falling of her chest, he'd think she were dead.

He bends to her. As he touches the metal to her skin, she opens her eyes.

"I'm just going to take a little listen," he tells her.

"Of course."

The doctor drops his stethoscope to her chest. Hears a rattle, like a coffee percolator. "Pneumonia," he says out loud. "You're clogged up."

Old Mrs. Gorkey, still looking at him, nods.

"We'll get you started on some penicillin. There are other tests I'd like to run. We'll need a blood–oxygen count. You ought to be hospitalized."

Mrs. Gorkey closes her eyes.

The doctor sits on the chair opposite the bed in the dim light of the room with his stethoscope in his lap. He thinks of a black turtleneck and maybe grey pants. That would look good. He'll go shopping after this visit. Maybe have Flury come with him, let him think he is playing a part. *What about this, then, son?* And Flury, seeing him with his greying hair and his double chin hidden would, of course, tell him he looked great. *Well, son, thanks for your help.*

That's what to do, thinks the doctor, leaning back in the chair, lifting his feet to Mrs. Gorkey's bed. Then afterwards he will write an article about their shopping expedition. "In these times of hustle and bustle, it's important for a teenaged son to feel involved in the occasional decision. Last week my son took me shopping after suggesting that I adopt a more casual look. He chose the black turtleneck I now wear with pride. Shopping together goes a long way toward building a strong bond between father and son."

Dr. Johnson scratches his thigh. Thinks of Flury, so grown up, close to being a man. He's managed in these difficult years to keep him busy and away from bad influences. The important thing is to keep a young man's hands busy busy busy. If they're busy, he tells Stella when she claims he is too old for making kites, then he won't have time to be touching the girls. A son needs all the parenting he can get. And he's committed. Entirely. Not like some people. Not like the old lady here.

The doctor leans forward, shifts his weight so that he is looking Mrs. Gorkey full in the face. He taps her on the shoulder. "Well, Mrs. Gorkey, you've just about managed to die. Just about managed to duck out."

She opens her eyes and smiles at him.

"I don't know what your game is. I really don't. But I'm here to say you took to this bed when your son needed you most. What was he, nineteen? Nineteen and you took to your bed."

Mrs. Gorkey licks her lips and says, "He can't have complete happiness until I'm dead."

"Now that's ridiculous. What kind of mother would say that?"

"A mother whose son loves her so much, he won't humiliate her."

"I don't understand you."

"Put it this way, doctor. While I am alive, my son cannot live his life. If he were to show his feelings for the woman he loves, if he were to open his arms to his daughter, he would humiliate his mother."

"You confuse me."

"What's so difficult? Gorkey refuses to shame me. As long as I'm alive, Gorkey bottles up his feelings. So my task is to die."

The doctor turns from the old lady. He simply does not understand her. How can a woman with a son she claims to love desire death? All this malarkey about living fully. A son needs a mother, and this mother, as far as he is concerned, bailed out too soon. "Quite frankly," says the doctor, "you're not making sense at all."

"That's because you're stupid, doctor."

"Better stupid than rushing to the grave." The doctor watches the old lady's face, considers his own will to live. "I'll tell you something. I'm living for my son. Simple. Right there in black and white." The doctor leans back in his chair, lifts his feet to Mrs. Gorkey's bed again. "He's my pride and joy, as they say."

The doctor opens the front of his suit and pulls out the cigar Jimmy Rolands gave him when Janie was born. Cigars are one of the boons of being a doctor. Yes! He enjoys a perpetual supply. He brings the cigar to his ear, rolls it between thumb and forefinger to hear the rustle of tobacco. "I am entirely committed to helping my son live his life."

"Which in my case means dying."

You are mad, he thinks, and half dead. "I think you're making a mistake. If you love your son—"

"I do. Your kind of love is a dangerous tether."

The doctor shakes his head. He leans forward and says, "In fact, excuse me while I quote myself, 'You can never love a child too much. Love provides the foundation upon which a child will grow into healthy adulthood.'" The doctor swings both feet from the foot of Mrs. Gorkey's bed and puts them on the floor, shifts his weight forward until his elbows are on his knees and his face is hanging over Mrs. Gorkey's. "Flury and me? A team."

He pulls matches from his pocket, lights his cigar, lifts his head to the ceiling and exhales. The paper birds spin in the purple-blue haze. Dust collectors, he thinks. Dust and damp and mites.

He looks around the small room. On the bedside table a catalogue lies open. The doctor shifts his weight and reads, "There are over twenty varieties of eggplant, many of which can be grown in your own home." The old lady, still reading produce catalogues.

In the days when the old lady worked in the storefront she kept a dusty pile of catalogues beside the till. The doctor recalls how she'd been thumbing through a catalogue the night Fran's daughter was born. It was the last night the old lady appeared in the store. Then she crawled into bed and stayed there.

"You prefer tomatoes or rutabagas?" she'd asked him. Or was

it artichokes? Some damn thing, some strange vegetable. Or fruit. She was always making nonsense conversation with him. Aubergine or avocado.

Again, the doctor looks at the article on eggplant. The writing is small, difficult for even him to read in the half-light. He looks at her sunken eyes, knows that after seventeen years in darkness, her eyes have grown dim. "You couldn't be reading this," he says to Mrs. Gorkey.

"I haven't been," she says.

"So?"

"Cora reads to me."

"I see. So where is she then?"

The old lady turns her head to him and smiles. "Up the hill."

"I see."

"*Do* you?"

"Yes. Keeps her out of trouble. Can't have her behaving like her mother. Like mother, like daughter."

The old lady lifts one of her hands, bids him with her finger to come near. "Like father, like son," she says to his face. Then she lowers her voice and whispers, "Have you heard? Charlie's back."

The doctor pulls away from the old lady's putrid breath, closes his eyes to her smile. Seventeen years ago she said exactly this to him. Seventeen years ago she stood before him and, with little hesitation, whispered, "Have you heard? Charlie's back."

~

"I'll just nurse Flury this once," Stella says, biting her lower lip. "Just so he'll stop crying."

The doctor refuses to let Stella nurse their newborn son. "No, Stella. He'll be fine. I know what I'm doing."

"You don't you how painful—"

"Shhhhh. Shhhhh. Get changed, sweetheart. Have a warm bath," he says. He wants to hold her, pull her close, but she is wet with breast milk. "Shhhhh, Stella. I'll take the baby. You have a bath."

"Just let me nurse him once."

"Listen, honey, I'm a doctor. I've been trained to know what's best." Flury, in the nursery, screams. So he turns from her, from her dampness, and goes to the child. He carries the taut arching body to the bathroom, where he runs water for Stella's bath. For a moment the baby is stilled by the sound of the water. He opens his eyes round, his purple lips forming a circle.

"There, baby, there," the doctor whispers until Stella comes into the bathroom in her housecoat, her belly still pouchy from the pregnancy. "There, baby, there," he says softly while Stella opens her bathrobe to get into the tub. He looks at her breasts. They are swollen and hard with milk. They are hot, he knows, hot to touch. Stella steps into the tub. She stands looking at Flury in his arms.

Flury arches his back, his arms flail and all at once from his tiny body comes a wail that briefly frightens the doctor. "What?" he says and looks to Stella for an answer. His wife, standing in the tub, milk dripping from her nipples, watches the baby.

He looks away. "Have a nice long bath, darling." He wishes as he closes the bathroom door that he had not seen her like that. "I'll run down to Gorkey's when you're through," he calls through the bathroom door. "Another kind of milk will do the trick." He sits at the living room window with the screaming child in his arms. He doesn't bounce him as he's seen Stella do. He does not want to spoil his child.

The sky is beginning to flush with the last hours of daylight. The child screams and he pushes the sound away, as memories of Charlemaigne crowd his thoughts.

Somewhere on the water.

*Can you smell the fish?* Charlemaigne sits on the motor, fishing.

The child stiffens again, changing the tempo of his cries. So the doctor jiggles the baby in his arms just a little. "There, there." No relief from the screaming, no brief moment of silence. "Quit crying, damn it," he says to the open and purple mouth. "You need a different kind of milk. That's all you need." The doctor moves into the darkening house to say at the bathroom door, just as nicely as he can, "Hurry up, dear. He won't stop crying."

No sound from within.

"Darling, please. He's still crying."

Nothing.

"Darling," he calls again. Flury blares against his neck.

"Go to hell," she shouts.

"Now, Stella, I am trying very hard."

"I said go to hell."

"Listen, honey. I'll get evaporated milk. From the store. So you've got to get out."

"You told me to come in here and relax and I'm trying to, but you won't leave me alone. Go to hell."

"Honey, that's not nice. I'm trying to help."

"Get lost."

He jiggles the baby, shouts over another piercing scream, "But he's crying."

"Get away from the bathroom door!"

He returns to the living room, trying to shut out the howls

of the child, longing to remember. But the baby cries too hard and really the doctor wishes Stella would just come out.

Which she does. Eventually. Stella swollen and not at all relaxed.

"I'll buy another kind of milk," he says to her after he's put Flury, still crying, in the nursery. "I'll go to Gorkey's. Right now."

Stella curls her fingers into fists and hits him, over and over, bangs his chest, her fists round and flailing and harmless, like Flury's. He grabs her shoulders, holds her distant. The front of her shirt is wet, her bound breasts leaking.

All the way to Gorkey's, alone in the hush of evening, away from crying purple lips, he recalls his last time fishing with Charlemaigne. *Can you smell the fish?*

~

He sees the huge summer moon rising. "Blue moon," he says and points, "on your shoulder." Charlemaigne, sitting at the back of the boat on the motor as though she's sat there all her life, turns to the moon, then back to face him. She leans her fishing pole against her shoulder, opens her arms wide and round to sing in a soft voice, "Blu-u-u-e moon . . ." Charlemaigne sings to the sun on the water and the moon on her shoulder. She picks up her pole and sends the spoon whirling through the evening sky.

"What are you using again?" he asks. He doesn't fish, though at twenty he should know how. It's on his list to learn. Doesn't know how to work the motor either. He's timid around water, will never dive the way Charlemaigne does, her body slipping effortlessly through the green water. He is useless too at helping to pull the boat up. Charlemaigne wrestles her small vessel through the mud at the shore, her toes gripping the slippery silt, laughing at the small and useless grunts he makes as he pulls the bow of the boat. But he comes fishing with Charlemaigne anyway. She is enchanting. "What's the name of the spoon you're using?"

"Red Devil," she answers, lifting her arm to the salmon-colored sky.

"Really?"

"Yup. The Pike Extraordinaire."

"Mmmmmmm."

"The Spotty Dick," she says and laughs, mouth so open she looks ready to swallow the moon.

He watches her and smiles. A perfect moment, he thinks. Charlemaigne on the motor, the moon on her shoulder. The sky so pink he could lift his hand and take the color home in his palm.

"Pike have sharp teeth," she says. "See here," she holds the Red Devil out for him to see. "No paint."

"Teeth?"

"Of course."

"Never thought of it."

"You would if one got its teeth into you."

"I'll never swim again."

"If you look down you can see fish."

"Then why can't you catch one?"

"You only catch one if it's stupid."

So fish, he thinks, leaning back, his legs extended, life jacket supporting his head, have teeth and brains. Mmmmm. Never crossed his mind to consider either in a fish. He looks up at the sky, watches thin ribbons of cloud lit by moonlight. He drops an arm, lets his fingers sink into the cool water. Spotty Dick, he thinks. Imagine comparing a spoon, a fishing tool, to male genitalia. Imagine any woman comparing anything to a man's privates. It makes him not uncomfortable exactly, but aware of his body, stretched out full-length like this before Charlemaigne, who could, right now, be thinking of his privates. He closes his eyes, imagines Charlie contemplating his body.

The water laps gently at the sides of the boat. He opens his eyes to watch Charlie casting. Her fishing pole is beautiful, even he can appreciate this. A fine-grained wood, polished and varnished.

"Nice pole," he whispers sleepily.

"I made it."

"Yeah, right."

"Did. Read up on how to make fishing poles, then went to the graveyard and found myself a tree. Why import split cane when there's wood in the graveyard?"

He sits up. "You didn't cut a tree from the graveyard?"

"I did. Willow. I peeled the bark, planed the wood. I made this pole."

"But Charlemaigne!"

"Charlie—I prefer Charlie. The flex isn't great. Weight reduction is a problem, but it's a start."

"You can't cut down trees, Charlemaigne. Not even willow. Not from the graveyard. You're not allowed to."

"Well, Edgar, I did."

"Charlemaigne, it must be illegal."

"Call me Charlie. The trunk was split in half, almost at ground level. So I cut half, left the other. With willows you can hardly tell, because there's still growth there. I cut it down at four in the morning."

"You cut a tree down by yourself?"

"For god's sake, Edgar. Yes, by myself."

"Whose grave?"

"My grandmother's. And just guess what she taught me."

"What?"

"Edgar, you worry me sometimes."

Edgar shakes his head. He lies back against his life jacket, stares straight up at the sky, thinking, I should not be out here with this girl. Then he moves his eyes to Charlie, looks again at her fishing pole and realizes that its beauty is nothing compared to her fine arms.

He stretches out a leg, touches Charlie's foot. Oh Charlie, he thinks, put down your fishing pole. "You're never going to catch anything." Can't she feel his foot?

"I feel confident," she says, her eyes on the steel-colored water. "I always feel confident when I'm fishing." Charlie's arms flex as she plays her spoon. The last of the sun outlines the muscles of her forearm.

"Stop now, Charlie." His feet are naked. He can feel Charlie's skin. He wants to touch her arms with his hands, wants to feel the flex of her muscle.

"In a minute. Oh god, Edgar. There!" She puts down her pole, stands in the boat. His body feels her shifting weight as the vessel rocks.

"What? Where?" He sits up, moves on his knees toward Charlie's standing body and as though thrust forward by the force of the boat's movement, he presses his forehead against her thighs. Warm.

"A painted lady," she says. "I swear I saw a painted lady." Charlie lowers herself to the motor again. Puts her hand against her thighs where his forehead had been. "You okay?" she asks.

He sits back on his haunches and looks up at her, the moon above her like a beacon. *This is the one. Love her, love her.*

"Oh Charlie." He puts his hand on her ankle.

"The painted lady. She's a clever butterfly, but I don't admire her."

He presses his palm against her ankle, moves his hand along the ribbon of muscle in her calf.

"Are you listening, Edgar?"

"Oh Charlie, I'll listen to you forever." And he rises to his knees, brushes his face along her thighs, his body lifting to her arms.

"What do you mean by forever?"

"Shhhh, Charlie, Charlie forever," his mouth lapping the inside of her elbow. "Can't you hear what I hear?"

~

The doctor nears Frank's Barbershop across the street from Gorkey's. He rattles change in his pocket, hopes Flury will take evaporated milk. Maybe he can add a tablespoon of corn syrup. He can't tolerate Stella's theatrics much longer.

Three old men sit on the bench outside Frank's, one leg crossed over the other, arms resting on their bellies. "Fine moon rising," says one, pointing to the moon lifting over Little Cypress Hill.

"Sure thing," says another.

The doctor pauses to look straight down Main, where the moon rises. He turns to look at Fran's window over Gorkey's General. Young Fran, face swollen with pregnancy, sits there. She too watches the moon.

"You'll have this baby very soon," he'd told her that morning.

"Soon. And you'll be fast. You've already started without knowing it."

The doctor considers the girl in the window. Thinks how she, so alone, gives face to all the girls her age who get into trouble that way. And there are more than anyone would ever expect.

Dr. Johnson swings open the door, nods to Gorkey, who leans against the counter, his arms crossed. The doctor knows that above, Fran sits waiting to have her baby and return to her family, still bleeding between the legs, her breasts still bound. The doctor rounds an aisle, wonders who will adopt Fran's baby. The Mooneys maybe. Or Riva Halvorson and her small husband.

The doctor walks the hardwood aisles, vaguely reading labels. Thinks of Fran's questions. "Will I see my baby? Can I hold it?"

"You might see your baby. But you won't hold him. Not a good idea."

"Does getting the baby out hurt like they say?"

"Mmmmmm. I suppose it could. But we won't let it. You have ether to thank for that." He told her ether would help her forget everything.

He finds the milk and a tin of syrup.

Young Gorkey slips behind the till, shifts his weight uncomfortably as the doctor says to him, "So how are you doing, young man?" The doctor thinks how blond men tend to be shy. Or perhaps, he considers, reaching into his back pocket for his wallet, maybe he resents being called young man. Gorkey, the doctor knows, is not much younger than he.

Behind Gorkey, his mother is a dim outline reading a catalogue.

"Hi there, Mrs. Gorkey," he says.

"Hullo, doctor. Listen, have you ever seen an artichoke?"

"No."

"Here's a picture. Maybe you've seen one and didn't know it."

"No, I've never seen one. Funny-looking things."

"Would you eat one?"

"No, I wouldn't care to try one."

"How about avocados? You must have had an avocado."

"Never. Thanks." He puts a bill in Gorkey's open palm.

Mrs. Gorkey rises from her wooden chair. "I have three in the back room. Three avocados. I had six, but I've eaten three. They came in a box from California."

"Oh. Really."

"Yes. I picked them up from the train station."

She was mad. Really. Train stations and avocados. "I see," says the doctor.

"So tell me. Do you prefer tomatoes to kumquats?"

"I've never seen a kumquat in all my life."

"There's a lot you don't see, doctor."

"Of course."

She moves toward him and glances at the milk and syrup under his arm. "Having trouble with that baby, I see."

"No, we're not. Just trying something different."

"So would you eat kumquats?"

He cannot see her features clearly in the dim light from the bulb hanging over the till. He hears a long moan from above.

"Fran?" says the doctor, looking up.

Mrs. Gorkey nods.

"Has she been at it long?"

"No. I'd say this is about the third we've heard, though she's been pacing most of the evening."

"She'll be out from under your roof soon by the sounds of it."

Mrs. Gorkey lets go her breath as the moan upstairs fades.

"It was good of you to have her live here. To employ her."

"She is a hand for us when we're short of them," says Mrs. Gorkey, putting down her catalogue. "She's a good girl."

The doctor glances at Gorkey. He notices a circle of wet around Gorkey's armpit and sees how he rubs his thumb over and over his palm. All at once, the doctor recognizes Gorkey's discomfort. To have a young woman upstairs moaning in the early stages of labor, a young woman who has paced all day like an animal looking for a place to birth. That would be enough to throw any young man off his mark. Enough to make a man sweat. Such sounds, that almost inhuman moan, are for women only.

Gorkey turns, sits in his mother's chair, crosses his arms over his belly. The doctor moves to the window, looks out at the moon and the men across the street who sit smoking, knees all in a line. Gorkey and his mother are quiet. They wait.

There. Another note from upstairs, a resonance spilling down, working its way like thin smoke. He watches young Gorkey rise to his feet, his hot eyes looking up.

The doctor leaves the window and walks to Gorkey. Puts out his arm, touches Gorkey's shoulder. "It's nothing to worry about, young man," he says softly. "It's just her time is all."

They hear another moan upstairs.

The doctor notes how the old lady moves her lips. She's counting. He and Gorkey watch, their gestures stilled. The moan slides deeper and gently dissipates.

"They're lasting longer," says Mrs. Gorkey. "She's speeding up."

Something in the way she speaks intimidates him. "Of course. I've got to get moving."

Mrs. Gorkey moves toward the door, "Yes, you'd better get on home and give some milk to that baby."

"Yes," he says. "Yes, thank-you."

Mrs. Gorkey scratches her thigh and pink-crested waves roll across the lap of her dress. She begins to say something, opens her mouth. Then her eyes fill with indecision and she stops. She scratches her thigh again.

The doctor waits, curious.

Mrs. Gorkey lifts a finger to him. Draws him forward with its movement. She opens her mouth and whispers, "I saw her at the train station."

He opens his arms. He has no idea what she's talking about.

She closes her eyes, leans closer. "Have you heard? Charlie's back."

At home the doctor boils water to add to the milk while Stella bounces the wailing child. He lifts the milk can to the neck of the bottle as she moves toward him, her eyes filled with anger. Then Stella pushes Flury against his chest and walks away. Struggling to hold the baby, he fumbles the milk tin and bottle. Creamy white liquid spills down the front of his shirt, his pants, the floor.

"Damn," he whispers to Flury, who's now wet with canned milk and milk from Stella's leaking breasts. "Stella, he's wet. No wonder he's crying. He's uncomfortable. You just change the baby, darling." His foot glides through evaporated milk as he follows her from the kitchen. "I'll have this bottle ready in two minutes."

The telephone rings. Stella narrows her eyes at him. "Stay out of my way."

"Hello," she says. "No, you may not speak to the doctor.

He's busy. Very busy. He's opening a can of evaporated milk for our screaming baby and then he's going to feed him. All by himself because he knows just how happy it will make the baby."

The doctor holds the wailing child in one arm and reaches for the phone with the other. "Stella!"

Stella turns from him, still speaking. "Then he'll put the baby down and although he cries the whole night, he'll leave it because Dr. Spock says we must leave my baby crying in the dark by himself."

"Stella, damn it!" And the doctor grabs the receiver from Stella's hand, pushes the baby at her.

"Hello," he says. He hears only breathing. "Hello, hello?" He covers the mouthpiece. "Damn you!" he whispers to Stella. "Hello?"

A moan. "Sorry, doctor. It's Fran. I . . . it must be time."

"Now just relax, Fran." He looks across the kitchen, sees the baby on the counter and Stella on the floor in a ball. "Fran, listen, I'll be there soon. Can you walk to the hospital?" Stella sits on the floor crying, the baby on the counter, unwrapped and screaming. "Listen, Fran. Just wait a bit. Call when the pains are closer. They're not close enough yet."

"What did you say?"

"I said call when the pains are closer. They're not close enough yet."

"How close? When should I call again?"

The baby arches his back, his small arms flail. "Fran, don't call. Get walking. I'll meet you at the hospital."

"When?"

He watches the rise and fall of Stella's back. She pounds her fists into the lino. "You go now. While you can still walk. I'll be by in a bit."

He moves to the baby, lifts him from the counter, places him on a blanket on the floor and crawls to Stella. "Darling. My darling, Stella." He moves his arms around her wetness. "Having a new baby is hard. No one said it was easy." He leans toward her, strokes the hair from her face.

She slaps his hand away.

"Stella, just settle down." He pulls away from her. The baby howls. "Stella, oh Stella," he touches her back. "Shhhh. Shhhh. It's going to be fine. Just fine."

The baby's crying changes pitch, speeds up. "Wa wa wa wa!"

"Damn it! Listen. I've got to go. Fran's in labor."

"I don't give a damn who's in labor." Stella uncurls her body and looks right at him. "You're not going anywhere until you feed this baby."

"But I can't. He's too upset." The baby's chest is the color of a stormy sky.

Staring straight at him all the while, Stella drops her housecoat from her shoulder, pulls at the binding until her right breast is exposed. "Well, I can." Stella reaches across the kitchen floor, drags the baby on its blanket toward her. She lifts Flury, about to bring his open mouth to her breast.

"For god's sake, not like that." Flury's open mouth at Stella's breast, wanting to suck and she so willing. "Not like that!"

"Go to hell," she says and guides Flury's mouth to her nipple.

The doctor leaves the house, slams the door behind him, turns his back on his home and his wife, who sits cross-legged on the kitchen floor with a baby at her breast.

He steps into the cool of the night and walks toward the hospital, where Fran labors. He pauses before the tree in Bruda's yard, every leaf lit by the moon. He turns into Bruda's messy yard. A tricycle. A doll on the lawn, her arms outstretched to the night. A toboggan on its side. Edgar Johnson, looking at the children's playthings, feels joy that he has a child who will one day have a tricycle in the yard. Hockey skates. Baseball gloves. And who knows, maybe he'll have a daughter too and his yard will be blessed with dolls. With that thought, he notices the eerie stillness in Bruda's yard, so black and white and motionless, as though someone had clapped and the children were lifted from their play.

But there in the garden against the bungalow is movement. Something white and swaying. Although the emptiness of the yard is haunting, the doctor cannot resist stepping onto the lawn to get closer. He steps over the doll, whose eyes stare at the stars. Baby's breath brushes his ankles, its impossible whiteness hovering like a chorus of spirits. He bends his body, moves his hand among the tiny floating blossoms. The feeling of loss which overcomes him is incomprehensible. Why such sadness? He has Flury, he tells himself. He has a son. He dips his hand beneath the tiny flowers and touches the dark stems.

Of course!

White reflects light, including moonlight. Just that simple. And dark is not reflected. Thus a floating appearance. A dark stem joining the seen to the unseen.

He kicks a piece of paper and feels very silly as he returns to the sidewalk.

The doctor speeds up, walks with purpose. He rounds the corner and without wanting to he recalls Mrs. Gorkey's words. *Have you heard? Charlie's back.* The doctor shrugs. So what? Why bother to tell him?

## A Fine Daughter

*Can you smell the fish?*

The doctor looks at his watch. How long now since Fran called? There's no saying, what with Stella on the floor like that and Flury alone and unwrapped, wailing on the counter. So difficult, thinks the doctor, to make Stella see things the way they are. If she could only have held out just one more hour. But there's no point thinking about it.

*Can you smell the fish?*

The doctor pauses, looks down at his shirt. Turns to face the moon. Yes, the front of his shirt is wet with milk, which, like the baby's breath, glows. Again the feeling of incomprehensible loss. "Damn it," he whispers to the night as he swipes at his shirt.

Dr. Johnson, closer now to the hospital, picks up his pace. Fran. How old is she? Seventeen, yes, young. She'll not need much ether. He considers twilight sleep, recommended by some practitioners because a woman still works to birth her baby. A combination drug, thinks the doctor, of morphine, phenergen and, perhaps most important, scopolamine. If he were to administer this to Fran, she would labor freely, would be active in birthing her child. She would push when he told her to. And best of all she would recall nothing. Nothing.

But, he thinks, stepping from the curb onto the empty road, with twilight sleep there are no inhibitions, and the animal nature of a laboring woman bothers him. Women in twilight sleep pace the floor, they scream and grope. More often than not they must be put in high-sided canvas-walled cribs to prevent them from doing damage to themselves, and generally they must be bound to prevent them from wandering the labor floor. Much kinder, he thinks, to use ether.

In front of the hospital the doctor plucks a poplar leaf from a tree, squeezes it, then reaches for the front door. But as he opens his palm, the leaf begins to unfold, shiny in the moonlight. He stops to watch.

"Butterfly wings are wet at first," says Charlie. Damn it. Charlie all over the place. *Have you heard? Charlie's back.*

"The butterfly looks a bit like this when it first emerges." She nips a poplar leaf from a tree, folds it in on itself, then holds it in her fist. "Watch. This is a butterfly just out of the cocoon." She releases the leaf on her palm, holds it close to his eyes. And he, mesmerized, watches the wings fill with the pulse of blood. He can, with Charlie at his side, see red and gold and veins running cobalt blue. He watches the butterfly's metallic pattern develop like a photograph.

"I see," he says and pretends to throw the leaf away.

Dr. Johnson, standing outside the hospital, recalls how, as he turned from her, she tapped him on the back. "That leaf, the one in your pocket, it'll dry up, you know."

The doctor throws the poplar leaf into the hedge outside the hospital. He begins to shoulder the door. Fran, he reminds himself, is a primipara. Her body is tight, muscles not yet softened by the process of birth. Primiparas, the doctor tells himself, pulling away from the door, can labor for hours and hours. Fourteen hours, thirty-six. It's not as though she's had two or three babies.

He pivots on his right toe and turns from the hospital to face the garden. But she was already two centimeters dilated this morning. He'd heard her rough moan, knew how she paced the floor.

The doctor turns, looks at his watch. 11:23. Call it 11:00. The uterus of a primipara is generally inefficient, unfamiliar with the rhythm of birth. Fran, thinks the doctor standing in the night, could labor for another ten hours.

He won't ring the doorbell, won't go in. He'll just walk past Charlemaigne's parent's home, see if he can see any sign of her being home, her fishing pole on the front porch, a pile of books in the window. See if old Mrs. Gorkey is right.

The doctor turns right at the Texaco. He can see Charlemaigne's parents' home at the end of the block. Charlemaigne was raised with three brothers, which is, the doctor believes, the cause of her foul mouth. She learned to fish from her grandmother but learned how to run a motorboat and refer to Red Devil spoons as Spotty Dicks from her too-loud brothers. He steps onto the grass, drawn to the single yellow light in the basement window. He can feel the dampness in the lawn rising to his ankles, dulling the polish on his shoes. He draws nearer, holding his breath and bending his body toward the light. There. Her head. Charlemaigne. *Have you heard? Charlie's back.* Yes, Charlie's back!

The doctor creeps forward, the smell of damp earth in the air as he nears the window. He pauses, hunkers down, folds his arms about his knees, ignoring the dampness at the seat of his trousers. Charlemaigne.

She has her back to him, her body curved intently over some small thing. In front of her sit several small vials and jars. Blue tape. Six or seven small sheets of glass. A navy blue box of cotton batting with a swath of whiteness pouting from the lid. A container of pins with red heads. Charlie lifts her arm to pull back a sleeve. He recalls the taste of sunlight, can feel the heat of her thigh on his forehead. Oh Charlie.

Charlie turns her head to read her watch. She is waiting. Timing, the doctor now sees, a slow flutter within the jar, a death.

Charlemaigne, he recalls, had to lie with her spine pressed against the boat's keel. If she wiggled beneath him too far from the boat's center, the vessel careened suddenly to the side, which made things awkward. He was concerned he might become disconnected from Charlemaigne. She said it hurt, and Edgar took that to mean her spine.

Edgar lifts from her dark triangle, looks up at the moon, then back to Charlemaigne. She pulls her shorts up, lifts her bottom to button them at her waist. Then she returns to the motor.

The water is still. Silver circles from their small movements spread across the blackness. She is quiet a long time, sitting on the motor, chin on her fist. The water moves like breath in a body.

"We should get in now," he says.

"You said forever."

"Of course. Let's go. It's late."

"Yeah, guess we should go in."

"That's what I just said."

"What if—"

"You won't be."

"Forever, right, Edgar?"

"We should row. The motor'll make too much noise."

Charlemaigne sits up straight, sighs against the darkness. "Did you know?"

"What?"

Charlemaigne moves her hand to her lower back, then leans forward to press her fingers against her tailbone. "If you look at the human embryo in the early stages of development, the tail is distinct. It's clear, very clear."

"What are you talking about Charlemaigne?"

"It's clear man descended from some creature with a tail."

"I know that."

"Yes, but we still carry our tails, Edgar, below the skin."

Edgar turns from Charlemaigne to look toward shore. Not far to paddle.

"By the eighth week it's gone. The tail's gone. But it's there in our memories. We absorb it, but it's always there, you see."

"Let's get in now, Charlemaigne." Charlemaigne is calling him an animal. Why else bring up the subject of tails? He recalls his moment of release and is ashamed of the guttural sounds he made. "Please, Charlemaigne, get rowing."

She looks at him. He watches her raised eyebrow against her dusky face. "Charlie, okay? Call me Charlie."

"It's late, Charlie."

"Move aside, Edgar."

He slides off the seat, inches along the bottom of the boat to the back. She sits where he has been, lifts the oars and, her muscular arms sweeping the air, dips and pulls the oars.

On shore she leaps silently from the boat, stands on the damp and slippery earth, looking at him. "Well?"

"Yes?"

"Get out, Edgar."

"Yes, of course." He stands. The boat wobbles.

Charlemaigne, clicking her tongue, stretches her hand to him. Lets him put his weight on her to step from the boat. He stands behind her to help pull the boat onto shore but slips in the mud, his bare feet gliding across the ooze on the shore's edge. He holds onto the boat and slips to his knees. Charlemaigne is in front of him, bent over, heaving.

He looks at her feet. Sees by moonlight how her toes bend to the earth, slide into mud, anchoring her. Charlie's long toes, he thinks, clenching, primitive.

His eyes move from the length of her toes along her dark legs, knots of thick muscle wander up her legs until he sees the black stain moving across her shorts. Charlemaigne's blood.

~

Dr. Johnson, stretched out on the damp grass in front of the basement window, watches Charlie. She returns to the jar, opens it and extracts the dead butterfly. Transports it to a bed of cotton and quickly spreads its wings. Drives a pin with a red head into the dark of the thorax.

The doctor pulls away from the window and walks slowly back to the hospital, thinking of Charlie the entire way. He pushes open the hospital door and makes his way to the delivery room.

The room is washed in the blue glow of moonlight. "Where," he calls out, "are the lights?" He hears a soft sigh, an airy laugh. He can smell blood's sticky iron scent. He fumbles his hand along the wall, finds a switch. Fran is on the floor, legs open, a baby curled in her arms. The cord, still not cut, loops away from her opening.

"Well," he says, "I needed a little light on the subject."

The nurse nods and backs away from Fran as he approaches.

"Came fast, faster than expected from a primipara," he says.

"No, I wouldn't call this a fast birth. She was over five centimeters when she arrived, and it's been four hours. The baby was born at 3:02 A.M., doctor."

The doctor looks at Fran. "I see." Then he turns to the nurse. "What's your name again?"

"Mailyn."

The doctor brings his hand to the side of his mouth, says in a low voice, "Now, Mailyn, primipara's are notoriously slow. However," he says, crossing his arms, "I neglected to consider her history."

"I don't understand."

"They wouldn't teach you this at nursing school, but experience has lead me to note that promiscuous girls have their babies fast."

"Oh." The nurse looks at the floor.

He arrives home in the early morning. Stella is sitting on the front porch feeding her baby a bottle. "He seems happy with the evaporated milk now."

"Yes," she says. "I nursed him for a while. And he slept. But woke me about three o'clock with these wonderful mewing sounds."

"That's nice."

"It's like his discontent vanished. You know, with the swing of a magic wand. Like in the fairy tales."

"I see."

"How was the birth?"

"I missed it." The doctor sits on the front step beside Stella.

"Oh Edgar. Surely the nurse gave her ether."

"Couldn't. But it happens, dear."

"Poor thing."

"It's too bad you didn't let me go earlier."

"Oh."

"Now don't you go blaming yourself." The doctor puts his arm around her shoulders.

"That poor girl. Who's going to adopt the baby?"

"Fran's keeping her. Foolish." He puts out a finger to stroke Flury's cheek.

Stella pulls Flury's blanket up about his ears. "I don't know why I acted like such a dimwit."

"Now, no more talk. Let's have breakfast."

He helps Stella to her feet. Takes Flury's warm body from her. Oh, the graceful bow of the mouth, he thinks, bending his face to Flury's, the sweet full scent of him.

"What did she call her baby?"

The doctor, pausing on the top step in the morning light, says, "I can't remember. Clara or something." He opens the front door for Stella. "Cora!" he says. "Yes, Cora."

~

Dr. Johnson pulls away from the old lady. Cannot tolerate her pungent perfume. Why he must sit in a back room of Gorkey's, listening to the whisperings of an old lady, he'll never know. Why whisper to him now, seventeen years later, that Charlie's back?

For the first time the doctor ponders just what information the old lady is party to that she should think he'd care one bit about Charlie's comings or goings.

*She knows. The old lady knows.*

The doctor looks across Mrs. Gorkey's body. Holds his breath as he realizes she could open her mouth anytime.

The doctor rises. There is some kind of plant on the other side of the bed. He could snub his cigar in the soil there. He moves across the room filled with the labored breathing of Mrs. Gorkey.

"No, not the plant. Please."

"What?" The doctor looks at her, but her eyes are still closed.

"Take it outside. Use it to cut the kite string."

She is mad, he thinks.

The doctor moves very quickly out of the back rooms of Gorkey's. He pauses near the Chore Boys and dishwashing liquid to grind his cigar out on the hardwood floor, then, having pushed the butt out of view with a polished toe, he moves to Gorkey to tell him his mother is fine. Just fine. "But she's lacking lucidity. Has for years. I wouldn't trust anything she says."

The doctor steps outside Gorkey's into the wind. People have gathered on the sidewalks as though waiting for a parade. The doctor hesitates, considers briefly that he may somehow have overlooked a town event. But no. There is nothing special slated on his calendar for today. Nothing at all. The doctor begins to walk up Main. He looks up at Fran's window and recalls, for some reason, her young face staring at the moon.

# The Old Lady

OLD MRS. GORKEY does not open her eyes to watch the doctor leave. Much better to see events as they occur behind her eyelids. She smiles to herself. So good to be in her mind, where memory is fine. After tracing memories for so many years, Mrs. Gorkey believes a pattern emerges and the future becomes obvious. When you can go back in time, it doesn't take much imagination to go forward.

She opens her eyes, turns her head to look out the small window. On the distant horizon, an orange glow. How remarkable, thinks the old lady, lifting onto her elbows to watch a thin undulating saffron line. Is this it, she wonders? Is this what she's been waiting for?

The old lady rises from her bed, and moves to the window to watch this dancing thread of color stitch her past to her future.

*Have you heard? Charlie's back.*

~

Seventeen years ago, as the doctor stood before her with a can of milk and Fran labored upstairs, Mrs. Gorkey knew that these words might put a daughter under her son's roof. Might bring a granddaughter to the foot of her bed.

She'd seen Charlie's hollow body curled on the bench at the train station the day Fran arrived. At first Mrs. Gorkey didn't know why Charlie's eyes were empty. She couldn't understand why a young girl just home from a long visit at her aunt's would look so sad. Didn't know why until she came home to the smell of lemon.

Gorkey in the kitchen of their back rooms, his hands still damp with lemon. Gorkey, his body big, but bigger now in his excitement.

"Gorkey," she calls to her son, "what's going on?"

Gorkey lifts his lemon-scented hands to her, his thumbnail carrying a fragment of rind. He lifts his hands and points upstairs.

She can hear water running.

She looks at her boy again. In his eyes the look of a child hiding a secret.

"Who's up there?"

"Come and see."

She follows him upstairs to the bathroom. He taps on the door, opens it gently.

There, in the bathtub, the young girl lies. Lemon rinds floating like stars against her nakedness. She moves a hand out of the water to her belly, places it there, upon her unborn.

"Hello," she says and Mrs. Gorkey isn't sure if she's greeting her or the baby.

The girl looks at Mrs. Gorkey. Her eyes are round, full as her belly. Then Mrs. Gorkey knows.

So when the doctor comes to her store the night of Fran's laboring, when he walks up and down the aisles like a man on the town, shoulders back, pink tie just a little off-center and arms still smelling of the newborn who slept and cried in his home, Mrs. Gorkey thinks of Charlie gone for almost two years and her body carrying the weight of loss. Mrs. Gorkey imagines Fran heading back to her hometown, eyes like Charlie's.

So she lifted her finger and beckoned the doctor. She hesitated for a moment, suspecting the power of her words. "Have you heard? Charlie's back."

She knew the doctor could not resist.

~

With the lovely golden line firmly in her mind, the old lady moves back to her bed. For the last time she crawls beneath her covers, folds her hands. She closes her eyes and watches the future.

The undulating line broadens, sweeping across the sky as it draws near. Wings, thousands of golden wings, churn against the blue.

Such beauty, thinks the old lady.

*Charlie*

CHARLIE SITS OUTSIDE the bakery on the bench up the street from Gorkey's, her knees wide. She has a butterfly net over her right foot and three apple strudels on a napkin beside her. She should have only one, she knows, but today she deserves three. Why she deserves three, she hasn't yet decided, except that it's already noon, so she could call this lunch.

The wind rips at the scarf on her head and blows road dust up her nose. It makes her thirsty, makes her want to wash her face and dollop on Nivea, makes her want to crawl under clean white sheets. But then, to be fair, thinks Charlie, transferring her strudels to the valley between her thighs, most days she dreams the crispness of sheets, pulled over her face.

Charlie believes that before death there is a brief drifting time, a moment on the reckless threshold where, still conscious, she will be free from wondering how the hair on the nape of her child's neck might smell. That thin line, believes Charlie, known only to mothers. She would prefer this state to death, dreams of arriving there without having to die.

Drugs could ease her into such a state. She appreciates this. But Charlie also knows that the doctor prescribes such drugs. She will choose the pain of thinking over a visit to Dr. Johnson.

So she continues to suffer thoughts of her daughter. She realizes that without drugs or death, she cannot stop considering how her daughter's voice will be deepening, will by now have the tone of a stormy sky. Charlie fears that her daughter yearns, in her body, for the slippery feel of trout, wants the weight of a fishing pole in her hand. Charlie fears that her daughter will never understand her dissatisfaction with lipstick and dancing lessons.

Charlie drops her head, plucks at a thin flake of strudel crust. That's the worst of it, her concern that her daughter, somewhere in her blood and her bones, has a need she cannot name. Has no affinity with Barbies or with painted doll houses and will never understand perfume or a new cashmere sweater.

Charlie picks up her first apple strudel. Damn the wind, she thinks as loosened sugar flies into her face. She could sit inside the bakery, move to a still place where she can eat her pastries. But there's something in the wind that makes her angry. And yes, thinks Charlie, opening her mouth to her strudel, how pleasant to be angry.

Charlie tastes apple. She has not bitten. Not yet. But this apple taste. Like apple pie in the sky. Charlie licks her lips and swallows. Apple of my eye. Old apples, new apples, ripe apples, bruised apples. Bruised-apple red. Like Fran's lips, seventeen years ago. A hot day. Fran's lips the only color on a white palate. She saw her before anyone else did, Fran a dot wavering on the silver tracks.

Charlie alone at the train station, curled up and holding herself despite the heat. The still air hanging over the tracks hot as the dickens. Charlie just back from a long holiday with her relatives, lies on the arrival bench for hours. No one knows she's back.

No one, except Mrs. Gorkey with her braid like a horsetail, her arms carrying a single box of who knows what from California. Avocados, thinks Charlie, all curled up and staring straight at Mrs. Gorkey. Charlie watches her braid swish as she drifts past, turns her eyes back to the dot on the tracks.

"Give your parents a call, dear," Aunt Penny had whispered to Charlie, who lay curled on the couch. "Let them know you're coming," her voice hushed as though she wanted Charlie to sleep forever.

"I wrote them already."

A lie. Charlie's alone on the bench, doubting her aunt's words. "Once you get back into the swing of things, you'll be happy. Two years away is long enough."

Charlie looks up the track, sees a hesitant dot meandering where the tracks converge. So Charlie sees Fran first, sees the girl younger than her with nothing other than a baby just about ready to be born and a made-up name on her bruised-apple lips.

Charlie follows her with her eyes for as long as she can without leaving her bench. Watches as she steps off the tracks, heads up Main Street, cradling her unborn baby with both arms.

~

Charlie lifts the apple strudel to her mouth, opens wide. It tastes good, very good. She ought to get up the hill. On a good day catching butterflies can stop the thinking. It's sunny, Charlie tells herself, despite the wind. So the heath fritillary should be out sunbathing in the heat. With her net she'll catch the sun-loving butterfly. Or maybe Cora. Cora on the McLellan stone like a butterfly.

Charlie brings a second strudel to her mouth. She can't think of Cora either, not today. Not in this raw wind. What is it like, she wants to ask Cora, to have your mother, your own mother? Some days she can't leave Cora alone, wants to sniff her skin, touch her hair.

Charlie has more than one secret.

~

After fishing under a sky pink as cotton candy, Charlie climbs in darkness up Little Cypress to the graveyard. Her back is bruised, the smell of Edgar clings to her body. His words, *Charlie, forever,* run over and over in her mind with the intensity of a night train. Charlie sits in front of what's left of her grandmother's willow and sees that, as she's given herself to Edgar, the rest of the tree is for him.

Charlie works most of the night. Cuts the willow, planes the sweet-smelling wood until it is smooth and shiny white.

"Well, well, Charlemaigne," says Edgar in the morning, "this is all very well. Only one problem. I don't fish."

"I thought you wanted to learn."

He looks at her for a long time. She watches his eyes run over the knots of muscle in her legs, up her thighs so she feels compelled to cross her hands, still holding the pole over her lap. He bites his lower lip, moves his eyes to her face and says, "No. You know, Charlemaigne, I don't think so."

She lifts the pole she's started for him in both hands. "What do you mean? What are you talking about?"

"I'm saying, Charlemaigne, that I think I'm finished fishing. Before I even began."

"But you've begun. You started already."

"No, it's not for me."

"What are you saying?"

"This is difficult for me, Charlemaigne. I'm saying I don't want to fish. I'm finished. Can I be any clearer?"

"Damn you. Damn you."

Charlie turns from Edgar. That night, in the light of the just-waning moon, she returns the wood of the tree to the earth. There, beside the newly sawed tree, Charlie plants Edgar's half-fashioned pole back in the ground.

Three months later, when Charlie leaves for her aunt's, the willow pole sprouts. Grows one branch, then another. In the graveyard.

~

By the time Charlie returns, the pole is a small bush. So Charlie catches butterflies on Little Cypress Hill. She thought she was brave to leave, brave to return. But Fran, thinks Charlie, opening her mouth for her third strudel, is the brave one.

Charlie looks down the street toward Gorkey's, imagines Fran sitting in the dimness on her three-legged stool. Charlie contemplates Fran's movements, sees her in the dull recesses of Gorkey's, stacking tin cans of pork and beans, Campbell's soup. Charlie sees the vegetables she weighs, imagines her polishing the keys on the till. Fran paying for her decision every single day.

Charlie swallows the wind, feels an envy that is like rage.

Charlie, her net on her shoulder, begins to walk against the wind up Main Street. She walks past the Texaco, keeps going straight. She detects a change in the light, as though a storm's approaching. The streets are busy. People laugh, shoulder one another. Charlie ignores them, steeling herself for the hike up Little Cypress Hill. She takes a deep breath, the air sweet as the apple strudel she's just eaten.

⌒

"Stick 'em up." A finger in her back, right between her shoulders. Elwood, she knows, without looking. She lifts her arms. But before she turns to face him, he's removed his gun and is hiding behind one of the gravestones. "I've got my sights on you. One move and you're dead."

"Okay, Elwood," she says to the voice.

Suddenly he is standing. He runs to her, his little fist tight. "I am not Elwood, am not."

"All right. Don't hit. Stop that!"

"Say it."

"Say what?"

"Say Davy. Davy Crockett."

"Davy," she says to the boy's face. "Crockett."

"Why, thank-you, ma'am. Thanks a lot." He lifts his coonskin hat and turns suddenly. "Shhhh. Cora's coming."

Charlie looks around. She can't see Cora, can't hear anything in this wind.

"Here. Get in behind me. I'll protect you," says Elwood. Charlie steps behind Elwood and crouches. Looks up at the sky and detects, in the distance, a strange golden line hovering on the horizon.

Cora appears like a vision, rolls like a cloud from the bushes. Charlie is drowning. She dips her head against the wind. Gulps once, twice. Again she smells the sweet air.

"I told you she was coming," shouts Elwood.

"Yes, you did."

Cora opens her mouth, but Charlie looks away from her, seeing Flury, the doctor's son.

Both of them watch his silhouette move along the rib of the

hill, kite under his arm, the wind lifting his hair. The tail of his kite flutters in the hot air, the green of Cora's ribbon snapping behind him.

Charlie looks at the distant churning on the horizon. And with unexpected clarity, she realizes she is here on this hill at this moment to take Elwood away. Simple.

She can feel Cora breathing hard in the wind. "I'll be off," she says to Cora. "I'll send Elwood down the hill too."

Charlie doesn't understand why, but she feels happy. She looks to the moving sky and drops her head to Elwood. "You get on down the hill, Davy Crockett. Please hurry. The sky is falling."

Elwood lifts his small face to the shimmering orange line. Charlie notes a moment of fear in Elwood's eyes and laughs. Ha! Feels so good. She hasn't laughed in years. Ha! "No, Davy, the sky isn't falling. It's just moving. Now get on down the hill. I hear your mother calling." She touches Elwood's shoulder, turns him in the direction of town. "Go," she says and watches him until he is well down the hill.

Charlie rambles through the bushes. Drives a straight line through the graveyard. "I never thought I'd see the day," she shouts to the roaring sky. "Hallelujah!"

*Flury*

FLURY WALKS ALONG the path that skirts the edge of the hill, not knowing until he sees her in the distance that he's been looking for Cora. She stands with the butterfly lady at her side, Elwood circling them.

Flury is disappointed. He was hoping, he realizes, to see her alone. He thinks that he intends to say sorry, but sorry about what? Sorry my dad has opinions? Sorry my dad knows so much?

Obviously, thinks Flury, he's not clear about why he intends to apologize. He just didn't like the look on her face when he admitted she was a topic of conversation. He wishes his father wouldn't have quoted Ecclesiastes, wishes he hadn't meant, "Like mother, like daughter." So he wants to make amends. But Flury isn't convinced he should be apologizing for his father. Maybe she *is* like her mother. He thinks he is definitely like his father.

He watches Miss Charlemaigne step closer to Cora. She stands very straight as though she intends to say something of great importance, dips her head to Cora's ear. And with her words, Cora lifts her head and looks directly at him. Despite the distance Flury swears that he smells her fragrance. Sweet and fruity. Watermelon and, though he has never smelled it, maybe kumquat. The citrus scent of tangerine.

He stops walking and stares at the threesome. Cora is still looking at him. Miss Charlemaigne says something to the boy, then starts to laugh. Even from here, with the wind roaring in his ears, he hears her laughter and is surprised by its richness. He knows this is a genuine laugh, not the sort of muffled chuckles his father makes as he reads the newspaper. Nor is it his mother's controlled hand-over-the-mouth titter when his father shares a joke. No, this is real. This laugh comes from the gut. It lifts from the butterfly lady's belly to her mouth and from there travels the air to tap and tinkle against his ear. Her laughter in the distance makes him feel like laughing too.

Flury begins to walk toward them. But just as quickly, the child scampers down the hill and the laughing lady turns and walks straight into the bushes, leaving him alone with Cora.

Flury nods.

She smiles.

He sets his kite in some nearby bushes. And his feet, affected by Miss Charlemaigne's laugh, move toward Cora, straight to Cora and her perfume.

Just as he approaches, the wind begins to stop. She takes her eyes from his face and looks toward Little Cypress. In her face he sees fear and, he believes, wonder. She lifts her hand and points. He should look, but can't. He hears her breathe, hears air move into her body and slowly out. He won't look. He can't.

"Flury, look!" She takes his face in her hands and turns it to Little Cypress. "Look!"

The sky is a roaring orange. Butterflies. Yes, the sky thick with butterflies. Orange as a river swollen with autumn leaves. A blanket of butterflies spreads over the whole of Little Cypress below. Terrifying in its beauty, the swarm churns the air, falters and lifts in the dying wind. Rolling forward, the thick band shadows the entire town. Below, the people of Little Cypress lift their arms to the swirl of orange. Their voices, filled with delight, rise up with the flickering of wings. Cora and Flury watch as the cloud gathers momentum, moves toward them.

Cora leaves his side.

"No," he calls out and lifts his hands to Cora, who runs from him toward an outcropping.

"Watch," she calls and hunkers down. The sky grows dappled, the sound of the wings above a soft roll of drums. He watches not the sky, but Cora. One after another the butterflies come to rest on Cora's still form, her slight body cloaked in pulsing orange.

All at once Cora stands. The butterflies explode from her long arms, her shoulders, cascade from her hair. Cora atop a large stone with the brilliance of a thousand butterflies lifting in waves around her body. A field of living energy.

Cora, with butterflies slipping about her, begins to move. He watches her uninhibited dance, Cora dancing for him like a river. Flury, watching her pure unrestrained movement, believes that until now, he has been asleep. The doctor's son steps toward Fran's girl, arms extended. Here, thinks Flury, is where I begin.

# *Charlie*

CHARLIE KNOWS she should hurry down the hill, away from Cora and Flury. But she is transfixed by the drama overhead. Standing on her grandmother's grave, Charlie sees what she knows can only be a miracle here in Little Cypress. She tries to focus on one butterfly, but it is like trying to follow a single snowflake in a storm.

Charlie turns from her grandmother's grave. She considers the knowledge of monarch butterflies, how a single migration from a region, which must be somewhere very warm, can take several generations of butterflies to complete. Clearly there is a knowing in these butterflies, some remarkable inner sensibility passed across generations.

Touching a willow branch, Charlie smiles at the crazy notion that her daughter might know the joy of fishing.

*Cora*

ABOVE HER, Flury closes his eyes. But Cora does not. She will not close her eyes to the thousand wings, translucent with sunlight behind them, glowing like tiny stained-glass windows. Cora wants, with her naked back pressed against a bed of wild sage and the stems of wind-stunted daisies, to keep each sense alive. Wants to taste the apple air, watch the play of dappled light on Flury's naked back. She lifts her hand, sweeps it along Flury's skin, soft as the wings of butterflies that surge around her. Cora thinks of Flury with flying in him.

Cora swallows, heady with the scent of apples. She pulls Flury closer. He dips his head between her breasts and presses against her. Her skin rises to his touch, and she laughs with the realization that all her life in Little Cypress has moved her to this moment.

"What's so funny?"

Cora pulls his mouth to hers. "Yes," she whispers.

"Yes?"

"Yes," she says, and in a powdered hush Cora opens herself to him. Only then does she close her eyes, hearing in Flury's quick breath the sound of wind and all it brings.

## Elwood

ELWOOD JUMPS from stone to stone, listening. The butterfly lady sent him down the hill. She wasn't exactly mean and her laugh was nice. But still, thinks Elwood, bending down to collect a stone, she's not his mom. She had no business telling Davy Crockett what to do.

*She's got folks pretty buffaloed around here. Rough and tumble, no holds barred.*

Sure thing, thinks Davy, gathering another stone.

*But she's folks same as anybody else.*

Davy shrugs. Time for a shooting match. He's got ammo. He stands with his legs apart. Beside him are Russel, his sidekick, and Bigfoot, the varmint who stole land from the injuns.

Davy glances over at Bigfoot, says, *Mighty fancy shooting iron for this part of the woods.* Bigfoot aims at the target. *Bang! Mighty fine shooting!*

Davy shoulders his musket. He bends to an outcropping and places one of the small stones he's gathered upon it. He lifts a big stone over his head.

*Better save your powder, stranger,* says Bigfoot.

Davy aims. *Crack!* He smashes the small stone. *I was afeared you fired too fast, Davy,* says Russel. *But you were dead center.*

Davy lets go another shot, this time aims upward.

He sets the sky afire. Brilliant flames lick the clouds and drop orange from the sky like sparklers. *I'm plumb flutterated*, he says to Bigfoot and Russel.

But they're gone.

He hears a sound like waves. Or is it laughter? He tilts his head, listens to the rush of sound. And that smell. He scoops handfuls of air to his face. Butterflies. He follows the sound of laughter up the hill, scooping air as he goes.

Later, in the growing darkness, lying in the bushes near them, Elwood tucks his coonskin hat under his head and begins to drift toward sleep. A butterfly lands on his head. Then another and another until they cover his entire body. Elwood thinks of his mother's laughing sunflowers and of butterflies whispering the color of the wind.

*Winnie*

NAKED, Winnie stands with her hands to the churning sky. She reaches up up. Wants to eat the sky. Wants to be more naked than she's ever been. She feels the wind peel layer after layer from her body.

A hand on her hip. Cool and shaking. She turns to Frank.

Winnie watches his eyes move over her body with fear and wonder. They pause at her neck. He says nothing. His eyes move to her dress on the grass, then back to her neck.

"You've still got your pearls on, Winnie."

She laughs and moves to Frank so he can unclasp her necklace. He glances again at the dress on the lawn, tosses the string of pearls on top of it.

Winnie, with the last of her costume glinting in the sun, moves toward Frank.

Frank begins to pull a sheet from the line.

Don't cover me, thinks Winnie.

But then he pulls another. And another and another until his arms are filled with billowing sheets.

Winnie laughs again while Frank spreads the sheets on the grass. Then, in the tangle of rippling white linen, Winnie straddles him. She grips his narrow body with her thighs, arches her back, looks up at the moving sky, watching it fill with color. When she closes her eyes, Winnie begins to fall through her body, like Alice through the rabbit hole. Down down she tumbles at first in darkness, but then in colors of cobalt blue and misty green, colors which become so intense they are almost painful.

Finally, with their love-damp skin drying in the breeze, she lies in Frank's arms and watches the sky wild with vermilion.

"Look, Frank. Butterflies. And look at you." She laughs. His cheeks are ruby red and shiny.

"What's that smell? In your hair?" he asks.

"Butterflies," she murmurs. "Or maybe quilts." And with that she decides to tell Frank everything.

*Fran*

FRAN SITS at her kitchen table, looking out the window. She should have unlocked the door of Gorkey's General by now, should have dusted the entire store and dealt with several customers.

But the movement of the long orange cloud keeps Fran waiting. She watches people below moving in the street, more people than usual for a midweek summer day. Still she waits. Her forehead to the cool of the windowpane, she watches as the shapes in the cloud become distinct and swarm over Little Cypress. She begins to laugh. This is what she's been waiting for. She lifts the window, thrusts her head into the wild air, into the velvet flight of butterflies.

With butterflies thick above her, Fran hears the rich voices of the boys below. "Love me tender," they sing sweeter than nectar against the rhythm of the sky.

Someone has opened a box, thinks Fran, and let joy out.

In the embrace of the love-me-tender day, Fran pulls her head from the window and moves toward the inner stairs. Like a bride, she takes them one at a time. She holds her breath, hears Gorkey around the corner, mounting the stairs careful as a groom.

Gorkey, arms open, pulls her to his chest, the chest she has not touched, not once even briefly in seventeen years.

"Mother's dead," says Gorkey.

"Yes, I thought so."

Gorkey lifts Fran's blouse from her skirt, runs his warm hand up her back. "I called the doctor again," he says.

Fran pushes her hips to his long legs. "When's he coming?"

"Now," he says, his hands circling the small of her back, desire burning in his fingers.

"Now? He's coming now?" Fran pushes against him, feels the heat of his throat from his open shirt.

Gorkey pulls Fran down onto the landing with him, his urgent hands discovering the skin above her nylons.

When the doctor knocks on the wall at the back of Gorkey's General Store, Fran holds her breath so her pleasure will not be heard. By the time the doctor rings the bell on the till, Fran's garters are swinging wildly against her thighs.

"The doctor has arrived," she hears him call as Gorkey's open mouth shudders against Fran's neck. "Damn it!" shouts the doctor.

By then Gorkey is able to call back. "Just a minute," he says.

# The Good Doctor

THE DOCTOR, hearing Gorkey's voice finally call out, is angry. Gorkey phoned him, didn't he? Asked him to come. He hasn't time to waste. He has no time to spare waiting on the general store owner while he does what ever general store owners do in their back rooms. "Damn it!" says the doctor louder. He will not wait another minute.

Gorkey emerges from the back. Out he comes with Fran, his cheeks as pink as the flesh of a watermelon. "My mother's dead," says Gorkey. And he leads the doctor for the second time that day to the old lady's bedside, Fran following.

The doctor watches as Gorkey moves to one side of the old lady's bed, Fran to the other. Both lean over the old lady, looking into her open eyes. And Gorkey and Fran lift their heads to each other and smile with a reverence the doctor is unaccustomed to observing. They bring their hands to the old lady's face and close her eyes. Fran rummages in the old lady's closet, pulls out a garish holiday dress and presses it into the old lady's folded arms.

"For the best avocado grove in heaven," she says and bends to kiss the old lady.

Enough, thinks the doctor, or he'll be here all day. He moves forward, signals to Fran to give him space. He looks along the old lady's arm, sees how the sapphire veins have, in the stillness of death, become the color of mulberry. But he is distracted. From the corner of his eye he sees Gorkey touching Fran.

The doctor lifts Mrs. Gorkey's skin. Lets it go. Watches it puddle against the bone. Where, wonders the doctor, is Gorkey touching Fran now?

He turns quickly. Expects to surprise them, but Gorkey merely rubs the small of Fran's back. Just as though, thinks the doctor, forcing his eyes back to the body before him, he'd been married to this woman for years, when really she is only an employee.

The doctor moves his hand to old Mrs. Gorkey's wrist, wills himself to consider her pulse, but he is startled by how Gorkey's long thin thigh presses against Fran's ample buttock. The doctor continues his examination, knowing that Gorkey's hips inch closer to Fran's behind, pressing more than his thigh against her. "For god's sake," says the doctor out loud, "you're distracting me."

The doctor intends Fran and Gorkey to leave the room, but they leave the store entirely. He hears the red front door of Gorkey's bang behind them. Why they would willingly step out into the street, the doctor cannot imagine. The air is filled with butterflies.

He sits beside the old lady, lifts his foot onto her bed. He stares at her for a very long time. Then slowly, certain no one is looking, the doctor leans over the old lady's face, lifts open an eyelid. Looks to see what Gorkey and Fran saw. He sees only himself. Ha! They'd seen nothing. Just their two faces together. One in each eye.

Finally the doctor lifts the old lady's hand, moves his fingers over her wrist and presses his thumb against veins, touches her fingers and, though there is no one to hear, says, "Yes, she's dead."

The doctor marvels, as he always does, alone with the dead, at the clarity of the moment. There's nothing complicated about death. Life is different. He is struck suddenly with the thought that he has known only once what it means to be alive. *Can you smell the fish?* The doctor brings both hands to his ears.

~

The doctor shakes his head, sees Charlie's arms, can smell the orchard of her thighs as he shifts on his knees toward her, his forehead pressing against her warm skin. He pulls her down to him, his hands feeling for the heart of the bold woman who fishes with such grace, who creates fishing poles from branches cut in the graveyard. He pulls her to him, puts his face against her neck and gently turns her in the boat, lays her against the boat's keel saying, "Charlie, forever." Quickly he pulls down her shorts, sees the bird's nest of his longing in Charlemaigne's exquisite body.

He breathes quickly, pulls his pants to his knees and pushes hard against her. He feels the heat of her body and in a moment is moving to the beat of Charlemaigne's heart, finding his rhythm in hers. "Shhhh, Charlie," he says for the second time. "Can't you hear what I hear?"

~

When the doctor emerges from Gorkey's General, the light outside is fading. He pauses briefly to look up Little Cypress Hill. Soon he'll be up there for another funeral. He peels a dead butterfly from the bottom of his shoe and begins the walk home.

Despite the hour the streets are crowded. All around him, people dance. He hears Sam Thomas's fiddle, the ripple of bow against strings. He scratches his head. What is the tune? Yes!

"The Devil's Dream." Fast, faster. He's obviously overlooked a town celebration. People whirl in the streets, their feet as light as butterfly wings. Bothered by the hoard of insects, the doctor begins to hurry home.

Howard, carrying his little boy, Elwood, in his arms, walks toward him.

"Well, well. There's a tuckered-out boy. A bit too late for a boy his age, I'd say," says the doctor.

"Yes, I suppose. We didn't mean for him to be out like this."

"Best to have a bedtime and stick to it," says the doctor. "Even my son, Flury, will stall if I let him. He's still playing games to stay up later."

"He wasn't stalling, doctor. We just couldn't find him to tell him to come in."

"You lost him?"

"Yes."

"A boy should come when he's called."

"We called, doctor, but he didn't hear. He was sleeping. I've just found him."

"Where?"

Howard points to Little Cypress Hill. "Up there. In the bushes."

"Well, you best get him home and into a warm bath. He'll be dirty. Have you noticed all the butterflies?"

"Yes! Oh yes. Lovely, aren't they?"

"They're dirty," he says and looks critically at the boy in Howard's arms.

"Of course, I'll bathe him."

"Good man!" The doctor turns from Howard, and, preparing to tell Stella he is exhausted, heads for home.

*Cora*

"AGAIN," SHE SAYS. She rolls onto her back and drops a raspberry into her open mouth.

"What?" Flury lifts himself on one elbow, startling the butterflies.

Cora turns to him, sees the look on his face and starts laughing. Her open mouth red with juice, the sound of her laughter melding with Sam Thomas's fiddle. "I mean, let's dance again."

Flury pushes Cora's shoulder. "Okay," he says and stands. He feels stupid, standing naked in the growing dark. Somehow, in this light, skin so startling white and smooth makes him believe his body glows. He feels like the white eggplant Cora tells him about.

"I forgot how," he says and crosses his hands over his nakedness until Cora's smile and the faint tune of a fiddle get under his bare toes and he starts to tap the earth. Finally he holds his arms out to Cora, touches her shoulders and begins to turn her in circles among the bushes. He turns her round and round in a dance step he vaguely remembers, and though Sam Thomas plays "Cock of the North," Flury begins singing in Cora's ear, "Round and round the mulberry bush, the monkey chased the weasel. Round and round the mulberry bush . . ." Flury steps away from Cora, makes sure she watches his eggplant nakedness. "Pop goes the weasel!" he shouts, and quickly thrusts his hips.

Flury drops to the ground, laughing. He has never done anything so stupid in his life. He has never felt so good. Flury, with his face pressed to the wild grass, Cora's butterfly-stained arms about him, is startled by his own laugh. Yes! He can do it, can laugh the way the butterfly lady does, hoot and holler until the back of his head hurts. The butterflies flit around them, and Flury laughs harder.

Cora pulls him up. She whirls against his body, her arms moving to the rapid notes whisking from Sam Thomas's fiddle. She turns toward the town, one long leg sweeping the horizon and then stops.

"What?"

"Look. Gorkey and Fran."

Flury looks through the tangle of branches down to the street, where Fran is in Gorkey's arms, their bodies pressed together as they dance. They are caught in an impassioned jig, reeling past smiling housewives, some with curlers in their hair, arms crossed over their bellies. Under the saffron scarf of the butterflies, Fran and Gorkey spin through groups of clapping old men and children, dogs barking at the blur of their heels.

"The old lady's dead," says Cora. She looks at her bare feet and pauses. "My grandmother's dead." A wild smile sprouts on her face. "I've never said that before." She lifts her arms, says loudly to the sky and the butterflies, "Grandmother!"

Flury isn't sure what to do. "She was *like* a grandmother to you."

She pinches his thigh. "Of course, doctor," she says.

"Stop it."

"Well, then wake up!"

Flury watches Fran and Gorkey below. "You mean Gorkey?"

Cora nods. Sam Thomas starts a new tune, hits the first sharp note. "You bet!" she says and lifts both feet, snapping her heels together.

"Really?"

"Yes!" Then, despite the music, Cora is still. She kneels. "The old lady saw this," she says.

"Saw what?"

"Us. Fran and Gorkey down there dancing up a storm. She was determined Gorkey would have this."

Cora bends to her clothes. Sits on the ground, begins to dress. She stands, pulls her underwear up and begins to laugh.

Flury watches Cora face the setting sun, hand on her belly, laughing. He wants to cover his mouth but cannot. "What's so funny?" he says, moving through the cool air to Cora, wanting to say something more.

She lowers her underwear, turns to show him her right buttock. "Here," she says. "I have a birthmark. So does Fran. We match."

Flury sees the birthmark but misses the joke. "So?"

Flury and Cora watch the evening unfold. As the sky darkens and only streetlights illuminate the scene below, they move down the hill closer to the light. The butterflies, without the sun to power them, fold their wings. Only then does Sam Thomas put away his fiddle, tuck his instrument into the tattered case and close the lid with the same gentle sureness as the butterflies close their wings. They watch children find their mothers in the faltering light, watch as one by one they are lifted into their mother's arms. "Shhhhh, shhhhh," say the women of Little Cypress. And slowly the men come to them, place their palms upon their backs and whisper, "Let's go now, love. Let's get home and put the babies to bed."

Watching this, Flury knows that such a life could be his with Cora. They could go into the evening and have a home to return to. He could touch her arm and say, *Let's go home.* There would be small children's bodies to carry, a bed to share. He and Cora could have this.

Then they see his father. See him step out of Gorkey's into the final dusk. The doctor hesitates and looks down Main Street toward the hill. Then he turns and heads toward home, stopping every now and then to pull a dead butterfly from the sole of his shoe.

Flury cannot stand to watch Cora go. Cannot tolerate seeing her white limbs slipping beneath layers of clothes without pulling her again to the ground. As his hand touches the nape of her neck, as his tongue inches over her skin cool from the night air, he tells himself that tonight his father will not check on him. Not tonight with the breath of ten thousand sleeping butterflies in the air. Not tonight with the stars dripping from the sky. Tonight, he tells himself with his face lost in Cora's hair, Doctor Edgar Johnson will not come into his room to check that he is sleeping. Flury wraps his arms around Cora, holds her, trusting that surely tonight his mother with a bit of fiddle music still in her legs will keep his father happy in their bedroom.

~

In the pink morning, Cora runs through Little Cypress. Flury, she knows, runs fearfully through the streets toward home, running against the growing light and his father's wake-up call outside his bedroom door.

But for Cora all the world is new. Golden light licks the tips of the rocks she passes. Sleeping orange butterflies glint from the leaves.

It's quiet in the golden morning on Main. Not a person in sight but Miss Charlemaigne, who sits ever so calm on the bench outside the bakery. Cora keeps her back straight. Presses her thighs together. Walks toward Miss Charlemaigne, hoping she won't know about Flury by the smell of her or the sway of her hips. Cora talks herself out of running, out of the thrill in her body but is certain Miss Charlemaigne knows anyway.

Suddenly, with the morning breeze wrapping around her just as Flury had, Cora knows by Miss Charlemaigne's smile that she doesn't care about the swing of Cora's hips or the smell of her, so she lets herself fill again with the need to run.

Cora runs past the Texaco and the coffee shop, leaping up and down, up and down the curb, startling sleeping butterflies so that a cape the color of tiger lilies flickers behind her. She runs with a rhythm in her feet all the way down to Frank's Barbershop.

Frank stands at the barbershop door, his cheeks pink as pomegranate, polishing his barber pole round and round, the colors so bright they make Cora dizzy. He lifts his hand to her. "Hi! Cora."

He isn't concerned in the least with Cora coming down Main in the early morning, hair dirty, knees stained with wild raspberries. He doesn't notice that she's hopping from curb to street with a cape of butterflies following her.

Cora crosses to the street to Gorkey's, steps into the yellow ring of a Hula-Hoop abandoned outside the storefront. She holds it against the small of her back, then swings it around her middle, lets her hips start circling round and round.

Across the street Frank begins to grin. "Can you believe it? Butterflies!" he calls, laughing.

Cora drops the hoop, smiles at him. "You're a nice man," she says and runs back up Main, then back down again, the brilliant cape flowing behind her.

Running, Cora recalls her mother's imaginary cape, remembers Fran in a pool of morning light, one nylon about her ankle. Cora lifts her arms to the morning sky and the trees along Main. Just below her mother's window, Cora lifts her face. "Fran," she calls aloud. "Fran! Gorkey!" she calls.

*Mari*

"ELWOOD, WAKE UP." Mari shakes his narrow shoulder. "Elwood, it's morning."

Mari fears that her son will wake laughing. She turns to look at his jeans lying over the chair, where she threw them last night. Wonders if the butterflies in his pocket still live.

"Come on, son. Up!" Not that laughing is a bad thing, thinks Mari, noting the sun on the sweep of hair. Not at all. But Elwood's laugh last night was troubling. So were his words. Howard was convinced Elwood was sleepwalking, but said ever so quietly that a visit to the doctor might be in order.

"Wakey, wakey, rise and shine," says Mari.

Elwood opens his eyes briefly. Mari can tell he is trying to move his arms. Then he is asleep again. But home. At least he's home.

Last night, when she couldn't find him, she feared she'd never see him again. But Howard found him eventually.

~

In the darkness Mari sees Howard coming up the path with Elwood in his arms. "Thank god. Oh thank goodness," she says, rushing to Elwood. She touches his sleeping face, swears she'll never let him out of her sight again. Mari dips her head to kiss her child, smells a delightful scent of apples. "You'll have to carry him to bed, honey."

"He'll need a bath first."

"For heaven's sake, let the child sleep."

"No," says Howard, shouldering the screen door, "He should have a bath."

"Why? It's too late."

"The butterflies. There were thousands of them. They've been landing on him."

"Good," says Mari. "Please take him to bed."

"Maybe they're carrying some kind of disease or something."

"Howard, put him in bed."

"The doctor said to give him a bath, so we should."

"But he's asleep."

"The doctor knows things we don't. Maybe the butterflies are just plain dirty."

"Can't you see your son's exhausted? Leave him alone."

Howard runs the bath. Sits on the toilet lid with Elwood asleep on his lap. He struggles to pull the boy's T-shirt over his head. "Where's his Davy Crockett hat?"

"Who's to say. Could be anywhere."

"Hope he hasn't lost it. He'll be fit to be tied without it."

Mari looks at her sleeping boy, begins to pull his jeans from his body. "Somehow I don't think he's going to care."

"Why?"

"I don't know. Couldn't say. Just something about him." Mari shakes his jeans to fold them, but with the shaking, butterflies fall from the pockets.

Elwood's eyes flicker open, and he scrambles from his father's lap, laughing. He stands naked. "Hello," he says and laughs again.

"Well finally, young man," says Howard, tapping him on the thigh. "Good to see you awake. What have you been up to?"

Elwood brings his hands to his tummy and laughs.

"It's not funny, Elwood. You had your mother and I worried sick. What have you been doing?"

Elwood turns to Howard, his laugh draining. He looks, thinks Mari, as though he is thinking very hard, as though he is struggling for words. "Listening to the butterflies," he says finally.

Howard looks at Mari, "He's just being silly, isn't he?"

Mari shrugs and watches Elwood circle the bathroom, whispering, "Milkweed white nectar listen. Hussshhhhh." His skinny legs bend until he is on the floor. Asleep.

"Man alive," he says. "If that isn't the strangest bit of sleepwalking."

"You think that's what it is?"

"Yeah. That was nutty. It's sleepwalking for sure."

"Oh?"

"What else?"

Mari shrugs. "Lift him again, will you?"

Howard lifts Elwood from the cold bathroom floor.

"Forget the bath, Howard?"

"I guess so. For tonight." He carries Elwood to his room and lowers him onto his bed. Mari pulls the blanket over his small naked body.

"I heard about this guy once," says Howard. "He sleepwalked like nobody's business. Got up in the night and shot his mother-in-law. It's true. And he got off because he wasn't himself. Now there's a thing for you."

Mari nods, says, "Goodness gracious." She turns off Elwood's light and follows Howard from the room.

Later, after Howard falls asleep, Mari goes into the bathroom and with tweezers, lifts the sleeping butterflies from the floor, drops them carefully back into Elwood's jeans pockets.

~

"Please, Elwood! Wake up." Mari can tell by the shift of his narrow shoulders that Elwood is waking. Please don't laugh, she thinks.

Elwood opens his eyes. Laughs. Then climbs naked from the bed and hugs his mother. He kisses her, then runs around the room. "Where oh where oh where?"

Mari stands, opens the pockets of his jeans. Elwood's relief is palpable as the butterflies flit from the recesses, flutter about his head in a circle. He dresses, says to her, "The sweet clover lover, over lover, over over."

Mari watches Elwood run around the room, butterflies following. She has two simultaneous thoughts. She needs to feed him breakfast. Howard will want to take him to Dr. Johnson.

*Howard*

THEY WALK to the good doctor's, Howard and his laughing son. "Just a little checkup is all, Elwood. Just to let the doctor have a look."

Elwood is quite happy with this, despite having to leave his butterflies at home. He runs and spins down the street, laughs out loud. Mutters.

What has happened? wonders Howard, watching Elwood, who stops to roll on the grass. Dr. Johnson, thankfully, will sort it all out. "Get up now, son. Right now." Howard can feel that he is close to shouting. "Please, son. Now!" Elwood keeps rolling.

Perhaps, considers Howard, he's had a bump. Hit his head on a stone. "Who knows?" he mutters.

"I do," says Elwood, who stops rolling.

Elwood walks at Howard's side, then bends to one of the many butterfly carcasses still littering the street. He picks it up. "Oh my lover over clover laps clover over over." Elwood places the tattered wings in his jeans pocket, then stops, turns to his father and waits to make certain Howard is listening. "Cora over over," he sings.

Howard shrugs. "Oh," he says. "Yes, of course." He gets embarrassed when Elwood speaks with such intensity; he doesn't know where to look or what to say. It is clear from Elwood's expression that Howard is meant to understand his words and to agree. "There's no doubt about it," says Howard.

Elwood nods quickly. "Round and round the mulberry, where weasel dances, and butterflies!"

Elwood lifts up on his toes, touches Howard's chest with the palm of his hand and with his strange eyes pulls Howard into a silent place, where for a moment there is no street or doctor to visit, only this warm hand, his child's hand pressed against him.

"Water water," says Elwood, "clover lover over, lover lap."

Howard nods. "Mostly."

Elwood takes Howard's hand in his and begins walking. "Mulberry, raspberry sweet and Flury."

Howard, with his son's small hand wrapped about his fingers, suddenly doesn't mind that Elwood is babbling. In fact, if he thinks clearly on this summer morning with butterflies glinting in the air, he quite enjoys his son's nonsense. As long as there is no one around to hear, he tells himself.

Howard is, in fact, happy. The reason, he concludes, noting the angle of the early sun on the lawns, is simple. He is happy because of Elwood's hand. Happy because his son took his hand. But when they get to Main Street and Elwood heads straight for Miss Charlemaigne, Howard worries. Hopes he won't start babbling in front of her.

Elwood stops in front of Miss Charlemaigne and stands. Miss Charlemaigne looks intently at him, as though telling him something important. They stare at each other for too damn long, thinks Howard. And he tugs Elwood's arm. "Come on, Elwood. Let's get a move on."

But Elwood moves closer to Miss Charlemaigne, touches her

thigh. She turns her head from Elwood and says to Howard, "Now here's a thing for you." She beams. "A father. A son." She looks closely at Howard. "There's nothing like a child."

Elwood reaches into his pocket, extracts the butterfly he lifted from the road. With tenderness he extends his hand and places the orange wings upon Charlemaigne's lap.

She smiles.

"Cora's got a baby," he tells her.

"Now, isn't that a wonderful thing?"

Howard pulls Elwood away and marches him down Main.

"Sounds to me like disassociation," says the doctor. "The mind separates from the body and a patient loses touch with reality."

When the doctor says this, all Howard can think about is Elwood's hand placing the butterfly on Miss Charlemaigne's lap. If that isn't the body acting in accordance with the mind, wonders Howard, what is? And he says so to the doctor.

"Now I'm not a psychologist," says Dr. Johnson, "but my bet is he'll need a little visit to the mental institute. I'll set you up an appointment with a specialist in Calgary."

"You can go straight to hell, doctor," says Howard, taking his boy's tiny hand. "You don't know anything about having a son."

*Cora*

CORA CAN TWIRL the Hula-Hoop forever. Sometimes the other girls drop out one at a time, slump against the pavement, breathless, as Cora whirls on and on. Sometimes they move together, drift alongside one another, lean against the window of Gorkey's, where Fran and Gorkey stand looking out. "Que serra serra, whatever will be will be," the girls sing.

Cora swings the hoop round her belly, but is not oblivious to Winnie, who stares from the barbershop across the street. So Cora eventually crosses the street to ask her for tea. Leaves are piled thick in the corners of storefronts, tucked in piles in the sewer grates and a wind smelling of winter opens the front of Cora's coat as she opens the door of Frank's Barbershop.

Winnie smells different. Winnie in the barbershop, her two girls gluing someone's hair on their Barbies, smells of something dark but not unpleasant.

Winnie in the barber chair swivels around to greet Cora. "Tea?" she asks. She lifts from the red leather chair, saying, "I'll be back soon, girls," although Cora hasn't yet invited her.

Winnie brings big crinkly leaves from wild raspberry bushes. She has them stacked one upon the other in a lovely pile, like slices of bread with a long piece of strawlike grass tied round them. "Boil some water," she says. Then she turns to Cora's window, looks to Main Street and the barbershop below. "You can see Frank so well from here."

"Yeah, you can. Mornings are best though. When he polishes his barber pole."

Winnie crosses her arms over her belly and says, "All these years. All these years and I've never watched him cut hair. Look," she says and puts her forehead to the glass, "look how he cuts. How intent he is. He's like a dancer." Winnie pushes her face closer to the window. "Look how he lifts of his arms." She wipes the gathering steam from the window and says, "The water's boiling."

Three leaves drop into the boiling pot. Winnie presses them down with a fork so the green rises in the water. "I collected these awhile ago. What with winter coming, I had to. There's enough, I think, to last until the baby's born."

Cora drops her hands to her belly. Still flat as a beach. She looks at Winnie, who's says, "Try to drink some every day. It'll strengthen your uterus."

Cora drinks the bitter tea across from Winnie at the kitchen table. She feels right drinking tea with Winnie watching, not saying much, the air around them soft as dust from a butterfly's wing.

When Winnie stands to leave, she lifts her hand to her throat, a habit of the body Cora recognizes from before. Then she notices Winnie is no longer wearing her pearls.

# Charlie

AFTER SCHOOL, Charlie sits on her bench talking to anyone passing by. Eats apple fritters between sentences. "Visit Winnie for your ailments," she says. "Colicky baby? Menstrual cramps? Flu or common cold? Depression or infertility? Winnie will help you. How do I know what Winnie has in her cupboards? Well, I'll tell you. I've been there. And being there tells you a thing or two. I went not too long ago to have my swollen ankles attended to."

Charlie takes a bite of her apple fritter, wipes her face with the back of her hand. "Winnie's cupboards are filled with dried plants, which she harvested after the butterflies came through. Now, you just listen to this," she says. "Winnie goes up to the graveyard on a full-moon night. She waits past midnight for the moon to steep in her urn of water and then uses this water to make her teas. She concocts all manner of things. I haven't an inkling what she put in my tea that day, humming along, dropping bits of this and that into boiling moon water, daisybane or golden rod, but I'm here to tell you it worked. The swelling is gone. You see, people have come to know the value of a visit to Winnie. Which gives good Dr. Johnson a little more time with his son.

"You would think that would make him happy, wouldn't you? Wouldn't you?"

*Flury*

CORA SITS ALONE on the top of the hill wrapped in a heavy pea-green sweater of Fran's. She likes the swelling of her tummy so much, is so delighted with the growing baby, that she wants to keep wearing her own clothes so she can watch them get tighter and tighter. But she's giving in. She has pulled her skirt over her knees to hide her legs.

Flury steps through the brown grass, the small pockets of snow, to join her. "So you're wearing Fran's stuff?"

Cora shrugs. She won't look at him.

Something's up, thinks Flury. Something is wrong. He reaches for Cora's shoulder. Cora turns from him. He sits in front of her, lifts her hair from her face, "What's up, Cora?"

Then he knows. She has something in her mouth. He can tell by the way her mouth is moving. "What is it?" he asks.

Cora looks at him.

"Come on, Cora, tell. What're you eating this time?"

Again she shrugs, her eyes saying, *I don't know.*

"What's in your mouth?"

Her lips pucker. She's trying not to smile. Cora lifts her brows.

"What's in there?"

Her eyes do a little jig and she turns her face from his, her cheeks growing big like a chipmunk's.

Flury pretends to ignore her. He hums for a minute, looking down at the town. Then quickly he turns his head round to hers. "Ahhhh!" he shouts.

Cora's mouth drops open. He watches, as she laughs and brings a hand to her lips. A golden liquid runs from the corners of her mouth, drops onto her skirt. "Oh god, Flury, you caught me."

"What is it?"

"Oh god, it's nothing. Go home or something." Cora licks her fingers, wipes her chin. "You're horrible," she says, bringing a finger wet with golden liquid to his face.

He ducks.

She wipes her finger against his neck.

"Cut it out."

"No," she says and brings her other hand to his face, rubs something sticky on his cheek.

Cora laughs, her mouth close to his ear, her breath curling candy-sweet across his neck.

"Cora! What the hell is it?"

She lifts away from him. Sits up straight, places her hands on her blossoming belly, waiting until he is watching and then "Ta da!" she lifts her skirt. An open can of Roger's Golden Syrup sits between her knees.

"You've been sitting here eating that? From the tin?"

Cora looks at him. "Oh my god, Flury, you look like your father!"

He sticks his tongue out at her.

She brings her hand to the spoon, doesn't care that she's getting her fingers all sticky or that the liquid drips from the spoon. She lifts it toward his mouth, and he pulls his head back and away, shifts his hands and finally falls back. He is lying down and she is above him with a spoon glinting over his face. The sweet taste of syrup drips into his mouth. Oh, it tastes so good.

"Stop it, Cora, stop!"

Cora leans over him. Puts the spoon on the earth beside her, then with her eyes still on him, puts her entire hand in the syrup.

"You're crazy," he says.

Cora lifts her hand and holds it against the sun, laughing. Her hand drips nectar.

He looks at the tin and at Cora, then rolls briefly from her to the tin. Dips his own hand, feels the thick liquid.

Flury frees his hand. Beside him Cora watches. His golden hand hovers over her thigh. Again and again he dips his hand, bringing the syrup to her body. She tugs her dress higher and slips out of her panties, shivering but wanting the impossible pleasure of syrup. Then he brings the amber liquid to the pool of her back, the mound of her behind.

"Oh Cora," he says. He looks at the wings of Cora's birthmark, magnified by syrup. Flury brings his hand closer to her mark and thinks of the long separation of Fran and Gorkey. He remembers watching families gather in the cool of the butterfly night. *Let's go now, love. Let's get home.* Words rising through the air to Flury, who, hearing them, longed to make them his. *Let's go home now, Cora.*

Flury moves his eyes from Cora's birthmark to her face. *Let's go home.* And Flury knows he desires life in the private rooms of Gorkey's. He wants the rich watermelon color of Fran's begonias in his life. Wants to know the curve of Gorkey's thumbnail and the paper birds he creates. He wants to laugh with Cora and feed her avocados, drop kumquats into her mouth. *Let's go home.*

Flury moves to his knees, glides his sticky hands over the baby beneath Cora's skin. He holds her face and says out loud, "Let's go home." And he won't let go of her face, won't drop his hands from her cheeks because he feels the muscles beneath her skin begin to flex and he knows she is going to laugh and he cannot say again, *What's so funny?* because this time he knows.

Flury will tell his father. He'll tell him and be done with it.

~

Flury, in bed, his blankets tidy about him, hears his father say, "Good night, son. Lights out. A growing boy needs his sleep."

"Dad?"

"What is it?"

"You've been up Little Cypress, haven't you?" Flury pulls at the corner of the blanket, rolls it between thumb and forefinger.

"Of course. I've been to every funeral up there for the past twenty-five years." The doctor smiles, puts his hands on his hips, "You know what, young man?"

"What?"

"I've got your number, oh yes."

He knows! thinks Flury. He knows what can happen on Little Cypress. Flury smiles back.

"It's not a sin, Flury, and I'm not angry." His father sits beside him on his bed.

The doctor lifts his hand to rub Flury's hair. "In fact, just the other night I was telling someone, Howard it was, that even you, at your age, do it. Everyone stalls. I stall. Your mother stalls. For some reason we humans will do just about anything to keep the lights on when it's time to turn them out." The doctor taps him on the head. "Little Cypress Hill though. Ha!"

He knew in his heart his father wouldn't have the imagination to appreciate what could happen. But Flury is determined. "Okay," says Flury. He's feeling brave. His father's playful. "Tell me about your first time."

The doctor jabs him in the chest. "Good one. That's good stalling material. All right."

"All right," says Flury. "Tell me, then, about when you first did it."

Flury watches as his father brings his hands to his ears, closes his eyes. Flury waits and after a time grows embarrassed to think of all that his father is recalling. "Dad," he whispers, shaking his father's arm, "tell me."

His father opens his eyes and blinks. He clears his throat. Laughs. "You won't believe this, I know you won't, but I can't honestly recall the first time with your mother. Oh Flury, life gets hectic." The doctor moves his hand to Flury's knee and squeezes it. "But this is an important topic, son. Just give me a minute. Let's start with the wedding."

Flury, listening to his father speak of a magnificent wedding, his wife's dress, her flowers and finally her transparent nightie, realizes that this conversation is not the opener to Cora that he thought it would be.

"I took her in my arms," his father says, "and her nightie, really, it was completely see-through, rode up her thigh." His mouth begins to pinch a bit here, as though it is sewn at the corners and someone is pulling the thread. "I rubbed my hand over her back and then her thighs. I believe we kissed for a while. It was all very pleasant, Flury." The doctor scratches his arm.

"Yeah?" says Flury. "And? Go on."

"Well, her nightie, son, continued to ride up her body, you see, and once it was up far enough, say just about breast level, I placed my penis in her vagina." The thread in the doctor's mouth is gone and he is able to smile. His mouth is free to open wide. His relief palpable.

"Wow," says Flury.

The doctor slaps Flury's knee and stands. "That's it!" he says.

"That's it?" says Flury.

His father lowers his arms and looks at him. "What do you mean?" He shakes his head, looking confused. Then he laughs. "Oh Flury, I'm sorry. I'm distracted. You thought I meant *that's it*, that's all there is to sex. No, not at all. I was thinking of something entirely different. I had an idea, that's all. As far as sex goes, well, there's much more. It's a very nice thing to do, so long as both parties are clean and respect each other. Very pleasurable. Of course, mother nature had to make it enticing in order to ensure continuation of the species." Flury's father sits again on the end of the bed.

Flury looks at the buttons on his pajamas. He doesn't feel as though he's got anywhere. "Thanks, Dad," he says.

"Sorry, son. I'm just too distracted to be much good at explaining sex right now. Your old dad's been shaken."

Flury looks at his father. Shaken? "What do you mean?"

"Well, I'm confused. Maybe I'm getting old, but nothing seems the same. Things are changing. I'm a little disturbed by a few things."

Flury shifts his legs, makes more room for his father. "Like what, Dad? What's changing?"

"So much. Too much. The list grows. Mrs. McRae. You know, she was such an upstanding woman. Involved in the church, on several committees. She was like a partner to me. And now? Bingo! A changed woman. Dropped her commitments like hotcakes, one after another. Put on her horrible skirts and started traipsing around the countryside."

"Oh," says Flury, "it's a change all right." He brings his hands to his eyes, wants his father to leave. At the same time he wants to touch his father's hand, tell him he'll stand by him. But more than anything, he wants to leave the bed, walk right out of the house and up the hill, where even now Cora might be standing on the McLellan stone, her voice wild as the stars churning over her head.

"It would be okay, Flury," says the doctor, "if Mrs. McRae went to the hills and stayed there, but she carries back all sorts of weeds that she feeds to the ill."

"I see."

"No, you don't. She gives them plants. Plants! Gives sick women plants she digs. Harkening back to a vile time, in my opinion. Dammit, Flury, what kind of example is she setting?"

Flury touches his father's shoulder. He's watched his dedication, knows his father's struggle to do what he thinks is right. "People forget, I guess," says Flury. "They don't remember everything you've done for them. That's human nature."

"Mmmmmm," says the doctor. "But is it human nature to tell your doctor to go to hell? Is it?"

"Who told you to go to hell?"

"Howard. Came in with his troubled little boy and when I gave my advice, he told me to go to hell."

Flury watches his father's hands sweep the wrinkles from his bedspread, something he has never seen his father do before. And watching his father's tidy movements, Flury hears humility in his father's tone, something, he realizes, he's not heard before or is ready to hear.

"He shouldn't have sworn at you," says Flury.

"Exactly." His father shakes his head. "The thing is, Flury, I don't think people's intent is to hurt. I believe something's changed them. Really. The whole town is different."

"Oh."

"Think about it. Have you noticed Fran's girl? That girl is pregnant. But where's the shame? Why isn't she off having her baby in some other town? Why isn't she intent on saving whatever face they have?"

Flury shrugs.

"I'll tell you. This whole town's turned so upside down they seem to accept this young girl's pregnancy. Why should she leave when everyone's pandering to her, dropping off silly little gifts and what have you?"

Again Flury shrugs. He swallows, his mouth dry.

"The point is, what's happened? Why would that girl be seeing Winnie when I'm here? I'm the doctor, aren't I?"

Flury nods. "You are, Dad."

"I saw her mother, had her in my surgery when others might have turned her away. I was kind to Fran when she came here pregnant and scared, Flury. She was frightened and lonely. I talked to her and took her interests to heart." The doctor opens his palms, looks at them. "I missed the birth, Flury, I'll admit that. Human weakness. Error. Call it what you will. I missed Cora's birth, but up until then the care I gave Fran was the best. Now this. It's like a slap on the face. Fran's girl marching past me to Winnie."

"Maybe she's scared."

"The point is, I don't think anyone is to blame. I think there's more at the root of this."

"Like what?"

"You must appreciate, son, that though I am a medical man, I'm also a spiritual man. I respect the unanswerable. I believe in the unexpected."

"And?"

"And I believe all this malarkey is the result of the butterflies." The doctor crosses his arms and sniffs. "There. It's said. It may sound silly, but that's when it all began. That's when things turned upside down."

The doctor smoothes Flury's bedspread again. "And I know someone who'll tell me all I need to know about the butterflies too. It came to me right in the middle of our little sex talk. That's when I said, "'That's it.'"

He stands. "Now, you've stalled me long enough." Then he winks. "And a good thing you did too. It hasn't been easy for me lately. It's good to have someone who understands."

The doctor stands at the door and turns out the light. "You mean the world to me, Flury."

"'Night, Dad."

"Good night, son."

Flury buries his head under his pillow. As if he would ever tell his father. Ever.

*Cora*

Cora pulls her skirt down over her soiled thighs and says, "So I told your father."

"No, you didn't. Don't you think your skirt is too small?"

"I like how I look. Anyway, I told him. Feels good. You were right to convince me to see him."

Flury won't bite. He's not in the mood for her teasing. She's so big it's impossible to sit beside her without letting the heave and roll of her tummy distract him. She should cover up a bit more. He shrugs. "That's good," he says.

"He won't leave it alone." Cora chews on a piece of spring grass. "He keeps asking, 'Who's the father, Cora?' The way he says 'Cora' drives me crazy. Why does he keep his lips all tight?" Cora lifts her other hand, opens her mouth.

"Would you quit chewing on that? You're always licking or eating or chewing."

"I'm hungry."

"Yeah, but do you have to sit and lick your fingers for half an hour after you've finished your chips? Try washing them."

"No sink up here, honey. Seen one lately?" Cora stands with some difficulty and pretends to look for a sink.

Flury looks up at her. Bare legs although it's barely spring.

They're purple with cold. He sees her underwear as she bends forward in search of a sink. "Okay, Cora, very funny. Sit down."

Cora holds her belly with one hand, lowers her weight to the ground with the other. "He was quite surprised," she says.

"Who was?"

"Your father. 'I have a nice family waiting for a baby,' he tells me. 'If you know anything about the father, it's good to let me know. In case he has diabetes or a blood disorder. For the record, you see. It's better for the baby.' So I told him," she says.

"No, you didn't."

"Sure."

Flury knows Cora has said nothing, but imagines his father's article. *My boy, the perfect teen, fathered Cora's child.* It would kill him. "You'd never tell."

"Like I said, he wouldn't leave it alone. 'The family who wants the baby needs to know,' he says again. So I figured, fine, I'll tell."

"You didn't."

"It was like this. Your dad said, 'I don't need a name, just any information you have. Think of the baby's future health.' So I looked all sad for the baby . . . and finally I just told him.

"He was a customer in the store, I told him. A guy just driving through on his own. He was older than me by quite a bit. Such a sad face on him. He was buying a Coca Cola, just to stop the thirst of driving. Remember, it was hot that day and the wind. Remember the wind. The kind that dried out the inside of your mouth if you opened it.

"The old lady was really sick that day, and beside the howl of the wind, you could hear her coughing in the back. So this man, tall, really tall, wearing a cowboy hat with grease on the band, puts his Coke by the till but keeps going back to the aisle with baby stuff. You know, the canned milk and Vaseline and what have you. He just stands there looking at the baby stuff until finally I couldn't take it, his eyes looking so sad, so I said to him, 'What's up, stranger?'

"I could tell by the way he turned his slow eyes to me that he hadn't realized I was even there. 'Why, hello,' he said and tipped his cowboy hat to me, which I thought was very nice.

"'You're looking sad,' I said.

"'Yeah, I'm sad all right.'

"'Mmmmmm.' I bent to the hem of my dress and pulled at a loose thread because I couldn't take his sorrowful eyes.

"'I had a wife, y'know. And a . . .' He couldn't say it. He was that choked up.

"So I said it for him. 'A baby,' I said.

"'Yes. He drinks that milk—that one there. Sweetest little guy you ever saw. Happy too. All you've got to do is walk into the room and his fat little arms go up and down as though you're the greatest gift ever. He makes all these noises, sweet little babbles and gurgles and all.'

"It was hearing him say 'babbles and gurgles' that got me going, doctor. I mean, that big man wearing a dirty cowboy hat gone all goofy in the second aisle, breaking my heart. I looked right at him. 'So what's the problem, stranger?'

"He pulled the cuff of his shirt-sleeve over his hand, brought it to his eyes and dabbed at them. I could tell from the water stains on his shirt that he'd been soaking up tons of tears as he was driving. 'My wife,' he said. 'She left me and took the baby. I can do without her. Fine without her. But the baby?'

"And you know, doctor, that man, he needed holding. He was

just so empty. So I touched his wet shirt-sleeve and said, 'You poor, poor—'"

"For god's sake, Cora," says Flury, "I can't believe the stuff you come up with."

Cora shrugs her shoulders, spits a fingernail she's been chewing onto the ground.

"And just at that moment, doctor, just when I touched his shirt-sleeve, the wind roared and the old lady coughed her last cough. And ten thousand butterflies fell from heaven. The light in the store grew orange, and his eyes, when I looked into them, glowed like coals after you've blown on them. 'I'll walk with you to your car,' I told him.

"So I followed him outside through the colored air, thinking all the while of the poor man missing his child. Any man, I thought, who could be so eaten up missing a baby must need comfort. And so when he said, 'You want to join me for a little spin?' I nodded. Slid in beside him.

"And you know, he gave me his Coca Cola. Let me drink it all without even asking for a sip. So we drove down Main through a wall of butterflies, kept right on going out into the countryside until we hit the pond where Miss Charlemaigne keeps her fishing boat. We stopped there, sat in the car and he told me his baby's name. 'Tim,' he said, slow and painful. 'Tim.'

"And his thigh, doctor, started shaking. I looked down, saw the muscle quivering under his blue jeans. So I lifted my hand to his leg. Set it on his thigh to still his shaking. Then he swallowed. I watched the rise and fall of his Adam's apple, watched it lift with the pressure of my hand and he said, 'You're a fine woman.'

"So I did my best to help him forget his lost baby. Tried to make him feel good. But after it was over, I knew he was still missing his child. And this baby, my baby, is going to be missed, is going to be a dark hole in someone's life.

"Your dad says, 'Cora, I'm here to help you. And in this case, helping you means helping your baby. I have a very nice home for your child, a good family who wants a son or daughter and can't have one. A child needs a mother and a father.' Then he wipes his nose with a handkerchief and kind of laughs into it. 'That man,' he says, 'put on a fine act to get you out of your underwear.'

"That's when I said, 'A big emptiness, doctor, missing a baby.'"

"Oh god, Cora," says Flury, "Why do you do it?"

"What?"

"He knows you're full of lies."

"So?"

"So it's a waste of his time. He's busy, you know. Doctor's are." Flury takes Cora's wrist in his hand, looks at her veins. Traces one with his finger up the length of her arm.

Cora sits with her thin wrist in his hand and says nothing.

"Hey, Cora, hey? You never told him that, did you?"

Cora lifts her head, takes a deep breath.

"Come on, Cora. Wake up." He shakes her wrist.

"I'm awake," she says. "But I'm thinking about the man."

Flury turns her hand over, thinking of her story as he drops his eyes to her naked thighs and her skirt, which does little to cover her. Thinks of how, even in her own mind, she made herself so easily available to a stranger. Yes, easy.

Cora turns then to look at him. "What are you thinking?"

"Not much. Maybe about my dad saying the family that wants the baby needs to know stuff." Flury, wishing she'd quit looking at him, recalls how she opened herself to him that butterfly day.

"I guess, as a doctor," she says, "it's his responsibility to get any information he can."

"You're right." Flury admires doctors. He will be a doctor one day. Like father, like son. "He's wise to find a family now. A nice family, Cora."

He hears Cora lift from beside him, and when he finally turns, all he sees is the back of her slipping between tombstones.

## Charlie

CHARLIE SEES HIM COMING, sees the walk that means business. She's been expecting this visit for some time. She sits on her bench and waits for the air to change. His appearance to her is like the sudden shadow that comes from a drifting cloud on a sunny day. The air begins to smell like water at the edge of the pond at the end of a hot dry summer.

"Nice day, Charlemaigne," he says.

She nods, corrects him for old time's sake. "Charlie," she says.

"Yes. Yes, of course. You still interested in butterflies?"

"Yes."

"Then maybe you can help. I'm curious, you see, about the orange butterflies."

Charlie leans back. "I'm hungry," she tells the doctor. Might as well get what she can from him.

"Mmmm. I'll buy you a cookie." He rises from the bench.

"I'm very hungry."

"A couple of cookies?"

"Sure," says Charlie. "The ones with candies. Make it an even half-dozen."

He comes back with cookies in a brown bag. He sits. "Here," he says, handing Charlie a cookie.

"You had a question?"

His hand bolts to the neck of his black turtleneck, pulls it up over his chin. He leans closer to Charlie. "The orange butterflies. I need to know about them."

Charlie takes a whopping bite of her cookie. With her mouth full, she says, "You mean the painted lady?"

He shrugs. "If I knew the name I'd be using it, wouldn't I?"

"Well, there's the painted lady. And you know, doctor, I saw one once from a boat. Under a full moon. I was fishing. I stood to point to it, made the boat wobble. That's when you ended up on your knees, remember?"

"No, Charlie. Don't start."

"Seems to me I pointed out the painted lady."

The doctor looks away.

"Like I said then," continues Charlie, "I'm not keen on the painted lady. She makes her way in the world through imitation. Those aren't her real colors. I think I told you this, didn't I?"

"Charlie, please. Stick to the butterfly."

"I've wondered what color the painted lady would be if she weren't so bent on survival. If the birds all took a break from butterflies."

"Another cookie?"

"Me, you see, I have seen my own colors. Saw yours too, Edgar. Learned them from the bottom of a boat."

"Would you just tell me about the damn butterflies!" He opens the brown bag by tearing the paper from one end to the other. He offers it to her.

She puts out her hand. "I saw you," she whispers.

"Butterflies," he says, leaning toward her, "Please, Charlie, butterflies."

"Heard you."

"No, Charlie, don't." He takes her wrist.

She pushes his hand away, moves close to him, her mouth almost touching his ear, her lips grazing his skin. "They'll have put her in a dress. Given her dancing lessons. But is she happy? What do you think, Edgar?"

The doctor tugs his turtleneck higher on his chin, turns from her.

Charlie looks at the empty sky.

The doctor begins again, slowly. "Charlemaigne, I want to know about the orange butterflies."

"Monarchs," says Charlie. "It was a monarch migration. Simple. *Anosia plexippus.*"

"Are you sure?"

Charlie nods. "Checked all the books. Kept wings from the migration. They match. Veins of the wings marked in black, large white dots speckling the black bands bordering the wing's margin. The color of the rest is reddish brown. Or, as you say, orange." Charlie stops to chew.

"Not painted ladies?"

"Nope. I thought so at first. Caught a few of the forerunners. I even told Cora that they were painted ladies. But I was wrong."

"So just a normal migration, you say?"

Charlie nods. "Yup. A normal migration. South in the winter. North in the summer." Charlie chews her third cookie.

"Tell me about migration."

"Well," says Charlie, "monarchs follow the same route year after year. They're believed to winter somewhere in the deep south, maybe even Mexico, but no one knows for sure. In summer they come north to feed on the milkweed."

"Same route, you say?"

"That's what they say. That's the thing about monarchs. None has ever been where it's going, but it knows how to get there."

"What?" says the doctor. He leans forward, lets his turtleneck slip from his chin.

"Start with a monarch born in the south. On the way to the prairies that butterfly gives birth to several others, right? It dies before getting to its summer destination." Charlie takes another cookie. "Her offspring spend the summer up north, eating and mating. So another generation of monarchs is born. When winter begins the great-great-granddaughters of the ones who began the migration pack up and go. They've never made the journey before, but they know exactly where they're going."

"Really?" The doctor pulls on the skin below his chin.

"Yup," says Charlie.

The doctor shakes his head. "Every year the same route, you say?"

"That's what I said." Charlie finishes her last cookie.

The doctor shrugs, quits stroking his chin. "You ever seen a migration before in Little Cypress?"

"Never."

"Thought you said they followed the same route year after year."

"That's what I said."

"So what, Charlie, were they doing here?"

Charlie shrugs.

"Why were they here, Charlie? Why would they be here instead of where they always are?"

Charlie brings her hand to her breast and begins to laugh. She gets up and leaves the doctor sitting on her bench.

*Flury*

WHEN FLURY OPENS THE DOOR to Gorkey's, the bell above the door rings. He lifts his hand to still the bell, looks across the till, sees Cora on her mother's three-legged stool.

Cora looks at him.

"Hi," he says.

"Hello."

He turns from her and heads toward the pharmacy shelf.

She follows.

Though he doesn't want to see her, he doesn't mind that she watches him. It's nice to have someone witness the importance of this trip. He's here to buy supplies for his father's black bag. "I want you to become familiar with the everyday contents of a doctor's bag," said his father. "The best way to do this is to begin with a few simple purchases."

Flury walks up the aisle, looking.

Cora watches.

He stands a little straighter. He's not buying Band-Aids. Oh no. Or cotton batting. No. He's here to get Dodd's Kidney Pills. He sees the small curved box and reaches for it.

"Got kidney problems?"

He turns to Cora. It feels so good to say, "No, I'm making

the purchases for my father." He rubs his hand over the top of the box, watching her face. He is terrified, suddenly, that she'll laugh. He sees the corner of her mouth twitch, and he drops his face fast. Silly girl, he thinks, turning from her heavy belly. When he came in, Cora looked just like Fran on the three-legged stool. Dull. Fat. Bored.

He shakes his head, laughs out loud. "Ha!" Who is she to laugh at him?

At the till he pays without looking at her. Puts the Dodd's Kidney Pills in his breast pocket.

"I've got kumquat here," she says.

"So?"

"Thought you might want to try one."

"No, I don't think so," he says.

"Why not?"

"Maybe before," he says, "but not today."

Flury opens Gorkey's door so the bell rings. Cora starts to laugh. He stands at the open door. "Okay, Cora," he says, "what's so funny this time?"

"The kidney pills. Try taking a few of those. They'll add color to your life."

"What're you talking about?"

"They turn your pee blue."

That was rude. He steps out of the store and walks down the street, feeling Cora's eyes on his back.

*Cora*

CORA DREAMS she is skating on the pond. The ice opens wide and she begins to sink, murky water ebbing into her skates. Water to Cora's thighs, the leather on her skates softening.

She drops farther. The pond tightens around her belly, and Charlemaigne, who rows in the distance, speaks. The rhythm of her words matches the stroke of her oars. On and on she drones, "You'll find Winnie in the graveyard. Oh yes. Winnie up the hill in the black night. Winnie under the stars, her hands picking cohosh and chamomile."

Charlemaigne rows a large circle around Cora, her words like pebbles. "If you were to shine a light on Winnie McRae," says Charlemaigne, "you would see her blouse. Such a lovely red, her blouse boiled for three days in the juice of rose hips. But she's there in the dark, Winnie is, the stars so close she can touch them."

Charlie's paddles dip. She is closer now. Silver water laps toward Cora.

"Must be black cohosh, not blue. Winnie knows black strengthens labor. Winnie knows such things."

Charlie's voice grows louder. "Winnie feels for the velvet lips of chamomile. Soothes the nerves. She'll boil it down, make a tea.

Pour it in the bath water when the pains pile up one on the other until there is no separating them."

The wake of Miss Charlemaigne's boat laps against Cora's belly. It curls about her and squeezes.

"Oooooohhhh," cries Cora.

*Fran*

THE WIND, thinks Fran, lifting her ear from her pillow, the wind caught in the awning over the storefront, moaning. She shivers in the dark, rolls against Gorkey. She presses herself to the rise and fall of his breathing, her forehead next to his naked back. So much holding to catch up on, she thinks.

The sound again.

Fran lifts her head to the darkness of the room, catches the last of the moan. She sits up, hears how it trails along the walls. Considers how the paper birds, which she cannot see, begin to stir with the sound's deep vibration. Then Fran realizes it is her daughter, not the wind, moaning.

*Cora*

WET. She is wet. In the dark, pulling from the murkiness of sleep, Cora realizes her waters have broken.

Cora swings her feet over the edge of the bed and with her damp nightie hoisted above her ballooning belly, she moves to the toilet and sits.

She feels another warm rushing and suddenly the weight within, without the buoyant liquid, seems very heavy. *Oh my god, oh my god, this is it. This is it. I am going to have a baby.*

A wave rolls. Cora catches her breath as it wheels round her back. She exhales as the clenching begins.

## Fran

So STILL IS THE NIGHT that Fran believes the earth holds its breath. From above, she hears Cora exhale a long rumbling moan, breath draining from her laboring body.

Fran, on her back, listens. "Your daughter's started her work," she tells Gorkey.

She shifts her hand to his naked thigh and presses, then brings her hand to her chest to feel the heat of Gorkey's body. Even after thinking about it for so many years, the very feel of Gorkey's skin startles her. She lifts a palm to the air and, in darkness so complete she cannot see her hand, moves it toward Gorkey's shoulder. She stops just inches from his skin, knowing his body by his heat.

# *Flury*

FLURY ROLLS OVER IN HIS BED. A sound, dark and rolling and warm. He shakes his head, feels the vibration in his chest. What is it?

Perhaps his father in the next room, snoring. Flury lifts his head from his pillow, tilts his head, wanting to hear clearly. No, it's not his father. The sound is deeper. He listens.

The low sound draws Flury. He tucks his hands between his legs, closes his eyes, feels the rumble deep inside his body.

# The Good Doctor

WHAT IS THAT SOUND? A cat in heat, maybe, crying for more. A female cat, thinks the doctor, can have a litter fathered by multiple partners. A litter of six with three different fathers. He abhors female cats. Why old Mrs. What's Her Name refuses to deal with the ungodly sound her cat makes in the night he'll never know.

Dr. Edgar Johnson holds his pillow firmly over his head. He can still hear moaning. Not crying and screeching, but moaning. Maybe not a cat in heat after all, but something similar and familiar to him. He's heard it hundreds of times. But can't, in this darkness, quite figure it out.

He hesitates, lifts the pillow from his face. Yes, he knows this sound. He sits up in bed while the deep moan fades.

It is the sound of mourning. Of grief. How could he not recognize it? And so the doctor, knowing someone somewhere is ill or has died, lies back down, brings the blankets to his chin and tells himself to sleep. Someone will call soon, and he'll need his sleep. All these years, he thinks, curling his knees into himself, of being up all night attending to birth and illness and death, have taken their toll. Taken a lot from him, he thinks, placing his hands, palms together, between his knees. He can feel it in his tired bones and in the very roots of his hair growing grey. It's in his eyes too with their dark circles.

The doctor pulls the blankets over his face and tries to stop thinking. But the thought of grief carries him to Gorkey and his strange grieving. Gorkey was excited after his mother's death. Gorkey pressing himself against Fran right in front of him while he checked for the old lady's pulse. While the butterflies flew over, making the old lady die. Making Howard tell him to go to hell and Winnie drop her commitments like dead flies. Turning a normal Davy Crockett-type kid into a crazed child incapable of communication. Making Charlie want to talk about the past he thought they'd agreed to leave behind. Making Fran's girl pregnant.

No. Impossible. In the darkness he returns his head to his pillow. He'll get to the bottom of this. He will.

## Flury

IN THE DARK Flury recognizes the emotion the moaning elicits. He shrugs the covers from his shoulders. The cry in the night makes him feel just as he did leaving Gorkey's last week, Dodd's Kidney Pills in his breast pocket, Cora's eyes on his back, her crazy laugh ringing behind him.

Flury recalls opening the door to Gorkey's, seeing Cora on her mother's stool, belly huge, her arms wrapped around the unborn child. And Flury knows that though he told himself she looked bored, what he saw was a wildness that frightened him. Nothing like the careful doctor who sent him shopping, who said, "I want you to become familiar with the everyday contents of a doctor's bag."

The sound circles Flury's room again, and he pulls the pillow over his face.

*Elwood*

DREAMING, Elwood wanders up and up a hill that is as high as the sky. His legs hurt, but he doesn't stop. At the top hears a sound so bright that it has no color, but he knows it has something to do with the baby in Cora's tummy.

He wakes from his sleep, climbs from his bed and wiggles his toes against the fluff of his rabbit-eared slippers. Then he shuffles to his window. Not quite light. Stars still in the sky.

*Mari*

MARI HEARS A LOW NOTE she recognizes but can't name. She sits up, tilts her head. She was asleep and hearing. It occurs to Mari that perhaps some sounds are discernible only when one is asleep.

Mari looks across the bed to Howard, who is curled like a child, his knees to his chest. It's possible, thinks Mari, that in sleep humans hear a different range of sound. Like a dog. Mari thinks of the high-pitched whistle some dog owners use. The kind you blow on and can't hear, but the dog comes running. You see, she forms the words in her mouth for Howard, when we are sleeping our senses are altered, like Elwood. His senses are keener.

Another sound, this time from Elwood's room. He's up. Mari hears him talk to his slippers, then hears the door slam. She looks across at Howard again. Good. He's still sleeping. She gets out of bed, moves to the open window, watches Elwood travel across the yard in the half-dawn in his pajamas and a sweater. Mari recalls the sound which woke her. "Is Cora having her baby?" she whispers as he passes the window.

Elwood shrugs.

Mari wants to follow, but doesn't. She blows Elwood a kiss.

## Cora

WHEN CORA OPENS HER EYES, pulls from the deep hurt, a hint of pink light hits the honey she spilled on the floor. For a moment she feels entirely normal, finally away from the intense gripping.

Cora lifts herself from the pool of honey, stands to retrieve her dried cold toast from the toaster. She pulls bits of crust away, watches them drop to the counter and feels a moment of panic. The pieces of crust on the countertop look like the path of bread crumbs Hansel left when his stepmother led him into the woods. She wants her mother. She wants Fran and Winnie here with her now. Cora doesn't want to slide into the pain and come out alone again.

She drops to the floor again, leans against the cupboard doors and with her finger begins scooping honey onto her toast. She sits with her legs open, contemplates the reality of a baby's head emerging. Yes. She feels as though she is turning inside out. She brings her toast to her mouth but cannot eat. Winnie, where are you?

She drops the toast on the floor. Moves to her hands and knees. "No, not again," she cries.

## Flury

FLURY IMAGINES he holds Cora in his arms. Dancing with her, he moves his hands across the pearls of her spine, believes he can feel the baby kicking. He notices the band of muscle tightening across her belly. He senses her gripping pain. He moves his hands along her spine to calm her.

In a room pink enough that he can just discern the rise and fall of his limbs moving, he recalls Cora saying, "I told him. I told your father." Flury pauses, his fingers spread along Cora's back, feeling the subtle shift of her spine as she breathes.

# The Good Doctor

THE BUTTERFLIES. The doctor knows he is on the verge of working out their strange visit. Monarchs. No, they were something else entirely. Otherwise they would have been here before. And he knows that when it comes to entomology, Charlemaigne is scrupulous. The doctor puts out his hand for his pocket Bible on his bedside table. The answer, he is certain, is there.

Before rising, the doctor dips his head under his covers. And certain that Stella, who could wake any time, won't see him, begins the exercises that prevent a double chin. Neck up, flex, relax. Neck up, flex, relax. And again.

Stella shakes his arm. "Shouldn't you be going?"

He's still holding his Bible. He puts it against his chest, looks up at her as she stands over the bed. She could do a few chin exercises herself. "Going where?" he asks.

"To the hospital. That girl's been in labor for hours. Haven't you heard her?"

"It's okay. They'll call when she's ready."

Perhaps, he thinks, he will suggest the exercises, tactfully of course, to her over breakfast. The doctor sits up, takes hold of his Bible and, without dressing, goes into his study. He has a bit of research to do first.

## Cora

THE LAST OF THE AIR in Cora's body drains from her. She is empty. With the air goes the pain.

She opens her eyes, dawn crawling under her bathroom door. The hushed breathing of Fran and Winnie in her tiny bathroom lit with candles. She is in the bath. She scoops water over her belly. In the water are tiny chamomile blossoms which rest on her skin.

Fran is at her side, humming. Cora can take the pain now, go into it. She can go anywhere it takes her, the crest of intensity tolerable because Fran and Winnie are here. Fran wipes Cora's face with a cloth. Without warning, Cora's thighs begin to shake, the water around her body quivers. Her muscles tighten and clench as she hears Winnie say, "It's time."

"We're not going to the hospital," says Fran. "Nobody's going to take Cora's baby."

"The baby's coming now. It's too late for the hospital anyway," Winnie with some urgency. She looks at Cora. "Let's get you over to the bed."

"No. Oh no no no." How can she move? How will she ever find her legs?

"Now listen, you can do it. Listen carefully. Bend your leg. Good. Now your other leg."

"I can't."

"Now, Cora, stand."

Fran dries her daughter's legs while Cora leans into Winnie's arms. Slowly they make their way to the bed.

# The Good Doctor

THE DOCTOR SITS in his study in his pajamas. He thumbs through his Bible. He is trying to concentrate, to find something which helps to make sense of what happened in his town, but is interrupted by the wail of the pregnant girl. Couldn't she stop, just for a moment?

The doctor crosses his legs and begins again. If monarchs always follow the same path, if they navigate north and south using some unknown method, but one which always puts them in the same place, then monarchs did not come here.

The doctor thumbs through Matthew, Mark, Luke. Nothing. On to the Hebrews, James, Peter, John. Then in Jude he reads, "For there are certain men crept in unawares, who were of old ordained to this condemnation, ungodly men." And later, "Likewise also these filthy dreamers defile the flesh, despise dominion, and speak evil of dignities."

The doctor pauses, holds his breath. "Behold, the Lord cometh with ten thousand of his saints, to execute judgment upon all, and to convince all that are ungodly among them of all their ungodly deeds which they have ungodly committed."

Ten thousand, thinks the doctor. Ten thousand of His holy ones. Saints and angels filling the air. Dr. Johnson lifts his head to the window, recalls the day of their coming, hears again the wings of ten thousand drumming against the sky.

The doctor stands. Saints, he knows, ten thousand of them, came to judge. He thinks of Winnie, Fran, Cora and even little Elwood. "These are murmurers, complainers, walking after their own lusts; and their mouth speaketh great swelling words."

The doctor is wet with sweat. He wipes his forehead. He brings his palms together and turns to his desk, picks up a pen and chews the end of it. Then he turns his head to the window and the growing light.

He has only a short time. He sits, drops his head to the paper and begins his article. He begins with Cora.

## *Flury*

FLURY MOVES AROUND HIS ROOM. He breathes Cora's sound, and when it's gone, when he can no longer hear her, breath drains from his lungs and Cora abandons his body. Flury is alone.

He turns, sits on his bed and shakes his head. He pulls his legs to his chest and wraps his arms around them. From the next room he hears his father cough, hears the hollow scratching of pen against paper.

Flury unwinds his arms from his legs and goes to the window.

Hormones, thinks Flury. That's all. Hormones making him believe he hears Cora. He buries his head in his hands.

What is it his father called it? Hormone-charged years. Yes.

Flury considers his father's latest article. "Joe Teenager will have a sense of security and well-being when he knows his parents genuinely love and care for each other. Husbands and wives who love each other as Christ loves the church have a sure foundation for parenthood. Joe Teenager may be creating parental challenges in his hormone-charged years, but parents, rest assured: teens gain security and their understanding of God's love from their mothers and fathers."

Flury stands at the window with his father's words in his

head. He contemplates not hormones but his parents' love for each other. Without wanting to, he considers his father's affection for his mother. When, wonders Flury, has he ever seen his father touch his mother? Flury begins to dress. Nothing about his father gives the impression that he has ever felt the way Flury has with Cora.

Flury lifts his kite from the shelf. He holds the thin skin of it between his fingers, thinks of his father's life, hears his father's words—like father, like son—and he reaches into his desk drawer. No, he thinks, this is not what he wants. He wants his body filled again. Carefully he slides a pair of scissors into his back pocket. Flury moves softly through the house. He steps into the morning with his kite under his arm.

*Elwood*

ELWOOD STOPS in front of Charlie on her bench, but Charlie's not talking.

"Wind!" he shouts.

"Yes," she says, but then she puts her finger to her lips. "Shhhh. Don't tell."

Elwood puts his hand over his mouth, wants to keep the word inside for Charlie. He shows her his hand over his mouth. He turns and heads for the hill. *Wind wind wind* in his mind even if his mouth's not saying it, all the way up the hill, where Flury flies his kite.

Elwood, hand over his mouth, watches the kite. Up up into the sky.

"Wind," he whispers finally. Another gust. "Wind."

Flury turns to look at him.

"Wind!" he shouts.

Flury nods, lifts his scissors from his pocket, holds them open to the kite string, then cuts.

Elwood watches the kite whirling up and up against the sky. "Wind," he shouts, pointing to Flury's distant kite.

In bare feet Flury runs to Elwood with thoughts of Cora flooding his head.

"Father," says Elwood.

Flury takes Elwood's hands, spins him round and round. "Yes . . . father. I'm the father."

"Wind," shouts Elwood as they turn to run down the path to town.

Flury holds Elwood's hand all the way.

# The Good Doctor

THE DOCTOR, walking to the hospital, pauses to look up Main Street toward the hill. He sees Flury holding Elwood's hand, running toward him. Elwood's in his pajamas. Hasn't he got a mother? Good god!

"Flury," he shouts, "let go of Elwood's hand."

"Dad. Hi, Dad!"

"Wind!" shouts the little boy.

"Dad, listen."

"Flury. Right now! Let go of that child's hand." He is infuriated. "And where, my son, are your shoes?"

"Wind!" shouts the Elwood, whirling as Flury lets go of his hand.

"Dad, listen. I'm the father."

"I've been listening. You haven't answered one question yet. Where are your shoes and what are you doing with this child?"

"I'm the father."

"Wind!" shouts Elwood.

"What are you talking about?"

"I'm the father of Cora's baby."

"Don't be—" the doctor hesitates briefly, then grips Flury by the shoulders. "You can't mean this. You'll ruin our family."

Flury nods.

The doctor, now filled with anger, pushes his face close to Flury's and whispers, "No one has to know."

"But I don't mind—"

"Be in my study when I get home," says the doctor, turning toward the hospital. "I know what to do. The town doesn't need to know. I'll be home soon."

"Dad, she's not at the hospital."

"Of course she is," he says.

"Dad," says Flury, "you're not listening."

But the doctor doesn't hear.

Elwood is skipping down the street toward Charlie on her bench. "Father! Father," Elwood shouts. He points back at Flury, who turns toward Gorkey's General.

The doctor enters the silent hospital. He scrubs up, thinking of the childless couples who will want this baby. He pulls on his gown. He'll make certain Cora leaves town. The girl needs an education after all. He'll pay.

He turns down the hall, his footsteps echoing. Turns into the labor room. Empty. She must be delivering. He lowers his mask over his mouth, and before opening the door pauses as he always does to prepare for the scent of blood, the sound of the last gulp of air before the final push. He swings the door open.

Silence.

Where, he asks himself, is Fran's daughter? He hurries down the hall, checking one room after another. The nurse follows him.

"What is it, doctor?"

"Nothing. It's nothing," he shrugs. Rushes from her and returns to the silent delivery room. He pats his empty breast pocket, leans against the wall, considers his article.

He thinks for a moment of the possibility that Cora has gone to another town to have her baby. But he knows that can't be true. It was Cora he heard in labor. *Dad, she's not at the hospital.* He sits on the delivery bed, thinking. He knows where Cora is. With Fran, who didn't do the right thing so many years ago either. Like mother, like daughter. With Winnie. With Flury, who turned toward Gorkey's General. Who will throw his life away if the doctor doesn't stop him.

## Cora

AN UNDERWATER FEELING, slow, so slow and calm. All Cora hears is her own breathing echoing in her ears. Between her legs, heat.

And again, rumbling up and over, a crashing white wave. *Push push.* Cora's body responds. She gulps air, holds it in, her body bearing down. Her thighs and toes and ears, the very back of her head, push to birth her baby.

Winnie, between her legs, her hands on the heat, eases back skin. Winnie between her legs, says, "Feel, Cora, feel your baby's head."

Fran takes Cora's hand, guides it to the heat of the baby's crown, the warmth making Cora whisper, "My baby. Hello, baby. Flury, our baby."

"Now, Cora, listen. Next contraction try not to push. We want to ease this baby out. Just breathe. Quick breaths. In your chest. Keep the work up top."

Pain is no longer a partner. She is on her own now, her and her baby. When the next wave comes, Cora holds tighter to Fran's hand, squeezes it. "Oh my god." Watches Fran's mouth telling her how to breathe. She mimics Fran's panting, resisting the need to bear down until the head of the baby slips from her body.

Cora pulls her wet hand from Fran's, hears a faraway echo.

What? What is Flury saying? He brings water to Cora's mouth.

A searing pain stretches the length of Cora's back. "I can't do this anymore," she screams. "Stop, Winnie, I can't do it, I can't."

"Yes, you can. Easy. Easy now."

Then Cora feels a sliding rush as Winnie calls out, "Reach down, Cora. Take your baby. It's here!"

Cora lifts a baby to her belly. Her baby. A wet lovely moving life. Warm blankets around both of them and in her arms a small rumpled body, a face purple as the dawn.

"A girl," says Winnie.

"Hello. Oh hello, my baby." Cora wraps her arms around her child's tiny body. "Flury, see." She takes Flury's hand and guides it to the baby's head.

Fran rubs the baby with a warm towel and laughs as the baby starts to cry.

"What's so funny?"

"She's got one too." Fran lifts the baby from Cora's arms and turns her. On her buttock, a stain like a tiny butterfly.

"Katrina," Cora says. "We'll call you Katrina."

# The Good Doctor

A LOUD KNOCK is heard at the door leading to the rooms above Gorkey's General. Outside, Gorkey's voice. "The doctor's here."

The door pushes open and Dr. Johnson strides purposefully across the room to stand in front of Cora. "Well, well," he says, "another primipara," his eyes moving from face to face then stopping at Flury. The doctor lowers his head to examine Cora then lifts his hand to the umbilical cord still running to the baby.

"Don't," Winnie whispers.

He turns to look at her. "Don't *you*."

Fran moves to the doctor and tightens her hand over his. "No. Leave it."

"We're not playing games here," says the doctor, but something in her eyes makes him step away. He walks slowly up the length of Cora's body. He looks closely at the baby, making a strange tick ticking sound. "I need to check the baby," he says, looking right at Flury. "Let's be sensible." He puts out his hand to pull the blankets from Katrina's body, but Fran pulls his hand away. "You're too late, Doctor Johnson, again."

# Little Cypress

FRAN RESTS on her three-legged stool behind the counter. Slowly, methodically she dabs lemon oil on the keys of the till, dusts round and round until they gleam. A long job, but mesmerizing. Pleasant, she thinks, in its repetition.

The awning over Gorkey's snaps in the wind. Fran lifts her head, looks out the window. Watches the scalloped edges of the awning ruffle. She puts down her dusting cloth, walks to the door of Gorkey's and swings it open. She sniffs the air. The first hot day of spring.

"Gorkey," she calls. "Gorkey, come here."

Gorkey, in the third aisle stacking tins of soup, hears Fran's voice. He waits until she calls again. "Anosia, come here," she says. He likes it when she calls him that. Gorkey walks to the front door, where Fran stands, a gentle breeze blowing her loosened chestnut hair. He steps out the door, his long fingers reaching for her hand.

∼

Frank, across the street, swivels his barber chair back and forth, back and forth. He's watered the geraniums that grow in the barbershop, washed his windows, cut three heads of hair and counted his money. Twice. Restless, he spins the chair around and stops when he sees Fran and Gorkey standing side by side in front of Gorkey's General, smiling like nobody's business.

He'll shine his barber pole, he thinks as he steps out the door. "Morning," he calls across the street. "Crocuses will be out soon." He recalls his conversation with Winnie last night.

"Do you know what the prairie crocus is also called?" Winnie had asked. "The windflower. It was used by Indians to ease the pain of childbirth."

Frank thinks Winnie will be out in the fields behind the house, looking for crocus, her fingers stained by the dark wet earth.

~

Up the street from Gorkey's, in front of the bakery, Charlie sits on her bench, Katrina beside her, feet swinging. Charlie looks at Katrina's hand, which is covered with melted chocolate. "Katrina, lick your fingers. I want to hold your hand." Wisps of Katrina's fine hair lift in the breeze. Charlie turns her face to smell the wind. She pulls Katrina to her lap, burrows her nose in Katrina's neck.

~

"Water water."

Elwood dips his hand into water, rolls his soaking sweet pea seeds. His mother digs a furrow for them, and Elwood drops in one seed after another.

"I still think it's too early, Elwood," says Mari.

But Elwood patiently sets the seeds in the row she has dug and pats earth over them. From time to time he lifts his head to the colored breeze and smiles.

"What are you smiling at?" she asks gently.

"The wind," he says. "Flutter up, flutterby."

"Thank-you," says Mari. Closes her eyes and imagines a shimmering orange sky.

~

"Higher. Hold it higher," Flury calls to Cora. He stands on the top of Little Cypress Hill, kite string in hand.

Cora lifts onto her toes, arms extended, holding a kite they've just made for Katrina to the sky.

He lifts a wet finger to the wind. "I'm going . . . now!" Flury runs, wind whipping his shirt tails.

The kite lifts, falters and plunges finally to the ground. Flury returns to the kite, lifts it in his arms. Barefoot, he moves to Cora, "It doesn't work. I expect it has to do with the weight of the tail."

Cora lifts her hand to his hair and laughs.

"What's so funny?"

"The kite's fine. Unlike her father, Katrina will have to learn to count to seven."

"What?"

"You ran on the sixth. The seventh gust is the strongest, remember?"

~

Flury's father is in his study. The heavy curtains are drawn. He hears a tapping on the window. The children again, he thinks. Again a tap. Finally, in irritation, the doctor rises, pulls the curtains aside. Nothing. It's just a tree branch in the wind tapping the window. But from down the street, the doctor thinks he can hear the sound of laughter. He pulls the curtains closed.

~

Fran shifts her weight. She leans against Gorkey. The wind is as familiar to Fran as Gorkey's breathing. The sound of the train rumbles in the distance. One of them will go to the station. One will remain to mind the store.

Gorkey lifts his hand to Fran's shoulder. "I'll go," he says. "You bring your stool out and sit here in the sun."

"No, I'll go."

"You just sit here, Fran. Got a couple of crates of tinned tomatoes due in."

Gorkey enters the store. Moves across the hardwood floor to the till. He opens the drawer beneath the till, collects the purchase orders. He looks up, sees Fran outside the window, standing in a pool of sunlight, her ample arms folded across her tummy. He loves the creamy dimples beneath the sleeve of her dress. His thoughts move to the pillows of skin above her hose, the indent the garter leaves on her flesh. Gorkey picks up the flower catalogue from beside the till, tucks it under his arm and moves to the door. He reaches up, flips the OPEN sign to CLOSED and steps outside.

"Let's go together," he says, taking Fran's glorious arm in his.

# Sources

Armstrong, Penny and Sheryl Feldman. *A Wise Birth.* New York: William Morrow and Co, 1990.

Cades, Hazel Rawson. "It's Up to You to Make the Right Moves." *Woman's Home Companion.* Jan. 1957: 90.

Gilbert, Eugene. "Gilbert's What Young People Think." *The Albertan.* 1957 issues.

Guitar, Mary Anne. "125 Ways to Stay on a Diet." *Woman's Home Companion.* Jan. 1957: 32.

Jordan, Edwin P. "Dr. Jordan Says." *The Albertan.* 1957 issues.

Strawn, Bernice. "Time is the Hardest thing to Manage." *Woman's Home Companion.* Jan. 1957: 70.

Tunley, Roul. "What Happened to Mrs. America's Bathing Suit?" *Woman's Home Companion.* Jan. 1957: 10.

Urquhart, Fred A. *The Monarch Butterfly: International Traveller.* Chicago: Nelson-Hall, 1987.

Weed, Clarence M. *Butterflies Worth Knowing.* New York: Doubleday, Page and Company for Nelson Doubleday, 1917. 10–11.